12/78

To Carol & Ken,
We hope you
enjoy the King Tut exhibit
and have a happy happy
holiday season AND a super
trip to California!

Love,
Jean & Fred

TREASURES OF THE
EGYPTIAN
MUSEUM
CAIRO

TREASURES OF THE
EGYPTIAN MUSEUM
CAIRO

Newsweek
books

New York, New York

TREASURES OF THE EGYPTIAN MUSEUM CAIRO

Editorial Director—
Carlo Ludovico Ragghianti

Egyptian Museum Cairo,
a volume from the series
"Great Museums of the World"

Texts by:
Sergio Donadoni

Design:
Fiorenzo Giorgi

Published by:
NEWSWEEK, INC.
& ARNOLDO MONDADORI EDITORE

Library of Congress Catalog Card No. 69-19066

© 1969—Arnoldo Mondadori Editore—CEAM—Milan

© 1969—Photographs Copyright by Kodansha Ltd.—Tokyo

All rights reserved. Printed and bound in Italy by A. Mondadori, Verona

INTRODUCTION

MOHAMMAD HASSAN ABDUL RAHMAN
Director

It is a great pleasure to introduce this book on the Egyptian Museum of Cairo, a museum that contains the world's most important collection of the arts of ancient Egypt. This primacy is a natural one, and I should like to summarize the story of the Museum and the efforts that have gone into its development.

Egyptian statuettes, stelae, scarabs and coffins often formed part of the curio collections of European courts and wealthy households in the seventeenth and eighteenth centuries. The *Description de l'Egypte,* the famous account of Napoleon's expedition to the Nile, aroused further public interest in Egyptian antiquities. Enthusiasm was heightened when the key to the decipherment of Egyptian hieroglyphics was found on the Rosetta Stone. The demand for Egyptian art continued to increase among collectors and museum directors.

In the early nineteenth century, under the reign of Mohammed Aly, the plunder of Egypt's art treasures was boundless. European consuls in Egypt, seeking to satisfy the requests of their countrymen — and perhaps not adverse to gain — became the first international dealers in the market. They obtained permission to ransack the ancient cemeteries, and their agents—from local families like the Yanni, the Anastasi and the Rifaud — were assiduous in collecting for them, year after year, whole caravans of valuable antiquities. In Egypt itself some twenty great holdings were formed in these years — including the Salt, Drovetti, Passalacqua, Anastasi, Athanasi, Thedemat du Vent and Belzoni collections — which were later sold in Europe and went to stock museums in Leyden, London, Paris, Berlin, and Turin.

Learned men like Champollion protested against the depredations and urged the Pasha to establish a system of control. In 1834 a service for the conservation of Egyptian antiquities was set up under Youssef Zia, and a museum was established in a school near the Ezbekieh Pool, under the direction of Sheik Rifaa, the Minister of Education. Youssef Zia and his assistants began to collect antiquities from the various archaeological sites, which were then being catalogued by Linant Bey to provide a check against appropriation of artifacts by tourists and dealers. But the museum was not enriched by Youssef Zia's finds, for most of the objects somehow disappeared before they reached it, or were distributed by the government as gifts to dignitaries and distinguished visitors.

What was left for the collection was so small that, when the museum was moved to the Ministry of Education's quarters in the Citadel, only one room was required to house it. There it was stored without a curator or a custodian. An important accession in 1852–54 consisted of the stelae discovered by Auguste Mariette, the French Egyptologist, in the Serapeum of Sakkara. The Archduke Maximilian of Austria, who happened to be passing through Cairo in 1855, begged Pasha Abbas to give him some antiquities: the Pasha presented him with the entire Citadel collection. Thus, the nucleus of a museum which Egypt possessed in the mid-nineteenth century can now be seen in Vienna.

When Auguste Mariette learned that Napoleon III was planning to spend the winter of 1857 in Egypt, he used his influence to secure an invitation. Although the Emperor's visit did not materialize, Mariette returned alone to Egypt. Napoleon recommended that Said Pasha, who was a friend of France, put Mariette in charge of a pharaonic museum. The Pasha's decree of June 1, 1858 appointed Mariette Director of Antiquities, but did not mention the establishment of a museum. Mariette was aware that if he pressed for a museum he would face the opposition of the dealers, the European museums — including the French collections — and the Egyptian government. He let the issue lie temporarily and proceeded to excavate a large number of sites. For the storage of the excavated objects he obtained the old buildings of a river-transport company on the Nile at Boulak. Mariette used four rooms to exhibit the most beautiful objects, and stored the other finds. He had the assistance of only one handyman, who made all the pedestals and cases. This small collection was so popular with the Pasha and the public that Mariette was able to greatly enlarge it. It was installed in a new building which was officially inaugurated on October 18, 1863 by the new ruler, Ismail Pasha.

Some of the new museum's pieces were shown at the international exhibition in London in 1862. In Paris in 1867, the best of Egypt's antiquities were exhibited in a specially constructed building — in the style of a small ancient Egyptian temple which was approached by an avenue of sphinxes. At the Paris exhibition, the Empress Eugenie was so impressed with the marvels of Egyptian art that she asked the Pasha to give her the entire collection. He referred her to the director of the museum, Mariette, who refused. Profiting from this experience, Mariette henceforth would not allow any of the museum's important possessions to leave the country. Only small objects and facsimiles were sent to the exhibitions in Vienna in 1873, Philadelphia in 1875 and Paris in 1878.

In 1878 the antiquities service became a governmental department under the Ministry of Public Works. Larger sums were allocated for the new department and the collection soon outgrew the building at Boulak where, however, the lighting was excellent and the exhibits were well displayed. Larger but not entirely suitable quarters were found in the Giza Palace on the opposite bank of the Nile, and the collection was moved there in 1891. The Egyptian Museum's present building at Midan El-Tahreer, inaugurated in 1902, was the result of an international competition. It was designed by the French architect, Marcel Dourgnon, in a Neoclassic style. In subsequent years, with the continuous influx of objects from new discoveries and excavations, the Museum again became seriously overcrowded. Eventually we hope to erect a new building with modern features, including anti-air-raid protection.

After the death of Mariette on January 18, 1881, his successors as Director of the Department of Antiquities were in turn Maspero, Grebaut, Jacques de Morgan, Victor Loret, Maspero again, Lacau, and Drioton. After Drioton, in 1952, Islamic and Coptic antiquities were united into one department under a native archaeologist who does not have to be an Egyptologist.

The chief curators of the Egyptian Museum after Maspero were: Lefebvre, Engelback, Mahmoud Hamza, Abbas Bayoumi, Moharram Kamal, Maurice Raphael, Victor Girgis, and the present writer, who is also the Director General of Egyptian Antiquities. The Department of Antiquities and the Egyptian Museum for a time were under the Ministry of Public Education, but they now are part of the Ministry of Culture.

While the collection was still housed at the Boulak Museum, the first guidebook, in French, was published by Maspero in 1883. The last of the four revised editions, in English and French, appeared in 1915. This splendid guide contained over five hundred pages of archaeological information, and conducted the visitor around the museum, room by room and case by case. The enormous subsequent growth of the collection soon made this method of presentation impractical: *Brief Description of the Principal Monuments,* the new guidebook which was brought out in English, French and Arabic editions between 1927 and 1938, describes the objects in numerical order and gives their positions in a list at the end of the volume. Besides the guidebooks, detailed descriptions of various categories of objects have continued to appear since the early twentieth century in the series called *General Catalogue of the Cairo Museum.*

The Egyptian Museum exhibits about 100,000 works, ranging from prehistoric times to the beginning of the Greco-Roman period. They are shown more or less in chronological order, beginning at the main entrance and continuing clockwise around the

Ground Floor, which is devoted to large works in stone, such as sculpture, sarcophagi, and stelae. The Central Atrium contains other large objects of mixed dates. The Upper Floor, reached by the southwest stairway, is also laid out clockwise and exhibits various categories of smaller objects.

Since 1952, the Egyptian Museum has developed considerably. Budget and personnel have increased, and various administrative projects have been carried out, such as the establishment of special registers for the six divisions — under as many curators — of the collection. The Mummies Room is now available to visitors, and the entire Museum is open every day of the week. Fluorescent lighting was installed throughout the building.

In 1960 a traveling exhibition of 119 items from the Museum, called "Five Thousand Years of Egyptian Art," was shown in Belgium, Holland, Switzerland, Germany, Sweden, Austria, Denmark, and London. The same exhibition was held in Tokyo and Kyoto in 1963. From late 1961 to the end of 1963, an exhibition of thirty-one Tutankhamon and three Twenty-second Dynasty items traveled to a number of cities in the United States: Washington, Philadelphia, New Haven, Houston, Omaha, Chicago, Seattle, San Francisco, Los Angeles, Cleveland, Boston, St. Louis, Baltimore, Dayton, Toledo, Richmond, and New York. In 1964 it went on to Canada — to Montreal, Ottawa, Toronto, Winnipeg, Vancouver and Quebec — after being shown in the United Arab Republic's Pavilion at the New York World's Fair.

Forty-five items from the Tutankhamon collection were exhibited in Japan (Tokyo, Kyoto and Fukuoka) in 1965, including works that had never before left the country — such as the golden mask, the bed sheathed in gold and the wooden chair with the carved, open-work back. In 1967 an exhibition of the Tutankhamon treasures at the Petit Palais in Paris drew a record number of 1,000,000 visitors. In Japan, however, the number of visitors reached an all-time record of 2,930,944.

The first illustrated description of the Egyptian Museum, by Mariette and Borchardt, dates from the Boulak period. More recently, in 1963, the Artia publishing house brought out another. This book is a welcome addition to the literature on the Museum, and will help to acquaint people everywhere with the great treasures of ancient Egyptian art.

Mohammad Hassan Abdul Rahman

THE ORIGINS

TERRA-COTTA VASE. *Fourth Millennium B.C.*

The development and variety of late Egyptian prehistoric pottery make it the most significant artistic expression of the period. This large vessel is a fine example of the dark-red ware, with black mouth and lining that lasted throughout late prehistory (divided into the Amratian and Gerzean periods) and continued in Nubia into historic times. Since they generally were not turned on a wheel, the contours of these vases are casual and irregular. The esthetic effect depends on the color contrast between the red, obtained with hematite, and the black, which is the result of a second firing of the edge of the vase. The absence of a dividing line between the two colors gives this ware its instinctive and spontaneous effect.

TERRA-COTTA VASE. *Fourth Millennium B.C.*

Cross-lined pottery — a red-ground ware with linear, often crisscrossed, decoration in white — is a product of the oldest period of predynastic times. Animal motifs were frequent; and aquatic species — crocodiles, hippopotamuses, fish — were often represented, as in this example. While the form is very free and exuberant, the decoration is highly formalized, with the rapidly stylized animal shapes arranged in clear rhythms.

Terra-cotta Vase
Amratian period; end of the
fourth millennium B.C.

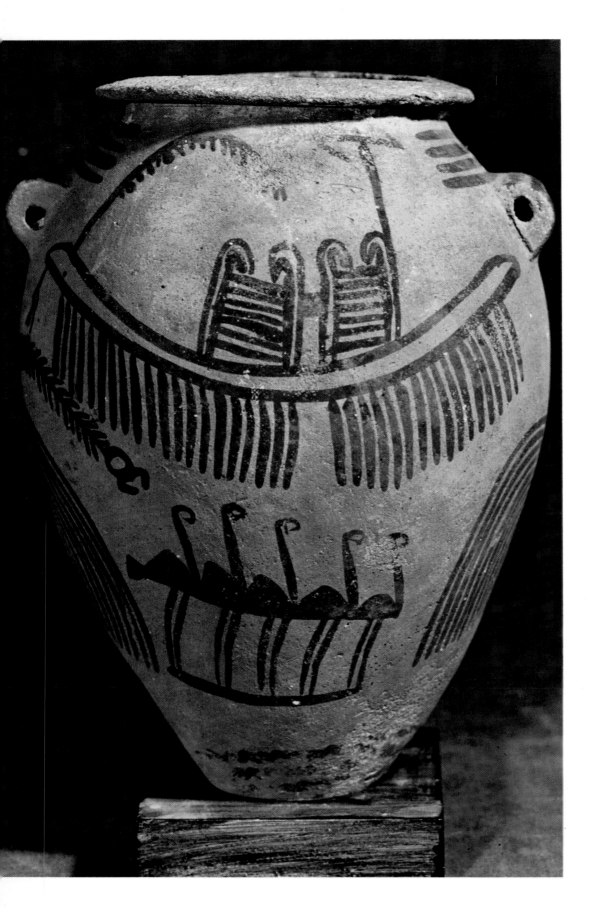

Terra-cotta Vase
Gerzean period; end of the
fourth millennium B.C.

TERRA-COTTA VASE. *Fourth Millennium B.C.*

The Egyptian artistic tradition of clear, analytical description within a unified and technically demanding structure began in the Gerzean period. At this time, during which the potter's wheel came into use, there was a radical change in ceramics. The color of the terra-cotta itself was often favored, decorated with a reddish varnish. There was particular interest in closed forms within well-defined elements: the base, the belly, the mouth, and the handles of this vase are clearly differentiated. The same forms used in such earthenware vases are also found in vessels of hard stone.

TERRA-COTTA VASE. *Fourth Millennium B.C.*

The elements of the later Egyptian figurative repertory seem to be discernible in this vase: exact architectonic structure, clarity of the whole form, an explicit descriptive function (antelopes on desert heights), and rhythmic repetition. But the similarities between an artisan tradition nearing its end and the intellectual simplifications of developed Egyptian art should not be exaggerated. The lack of an inner dynamism in early works of this type deprives them of the contained warmth characteristic of the classical art of Egypt.

Terra-cotta Vase
Gerzean period; end of the
fourth millennium B.C.

TERRA-COTTA VASE. *Fourth Millennium B.C.*

Gerzean vases have a typical form, as well as a distinctive decoration, that is more varied than the Amratian. As in this example, they often feature boats with cabins and oars, human figures (here a dancing woman flanked by two men), and stylized animals (note the lyre-shaped horns). The concern with descriptive detail somewhat compromises the decorative scheme, and the various representations are not always readily interrelated. This is all the more true since some elements are obviously "fillers" (i.e. the groups of zigzag lines perhaps representing water, and the rows of "Z's") that show a disregard for background independent of the decoration — an attitude that is generally alien to classical Egyptian art.

Terra-cotta Vase
Gerzean period; end of the
fourth millennium B.C.

Right: detail of the decoration.

PLUNDERED ANIMALS AND TREES. *Circa 3200 B.C.*

This is the lower part of an object similar to the *Palette of Narmer* (page 26). It is a large reproduction of a palette for grinding and kneeding antimony — which was utilized as eye shadow — with an elaboration of decoration unknown in the models in daily use. This explains the hollow on one of the sides, which serves only as an excuse for various decorative arrangements. Because of the votive function of such objects, their decorations often represent religious ceremonies. Here the rows of animals and the group of trees probably represent booty whose origin (Libya?) is perhaps given by the hieroglyphic below. The clarity of the register-system composition, as if laying out the contents of a catalogue, suggests the taste for rationalism and order that underlies the evident ability in composition and execution. This element of logic is enlivened by the stylized vitality of the figures. Such details as the ram on the left, who turns to look at the land it is leaving, prevent the repetition of animals from becoming mechanical. This palette is an early example of the balance between abstract structure and feeling for life that is typical of the art that may more properly be called Egyptian.

Plundered Animals and Trees
Votive palette.
Predynastic period; circa 3200 B.C.
Carved schist; height 11 3/4".
From Abydos.

THE KING REPRESENTED IN ANIMAL FORMS, DESTROYING CITIES. *Circa 3200 B.C.*

This is the reverse side, or face, of the preceding palette. The commemorative nature of the work is even more apparent here. It records a victory of the "Scorpion King," who is shown as a scorpion and as other royal animals (the falcon, the two-falcons and the lion). In his successive guises, the King dismantles with a mattock seven fortified city walls — shown conventionally in plan — within which are the bricks that have fallen under the blows, and the name of the city. The scene may actually represent seven different cities, or it may be only one city (perhaps Buto) which is given a different epithet each time it is shown. This would make a parallel between the sovereign with seven names and the city that he destroys under its seven designations. This side, more markedly than the other, is a pictogram rather than a proper representation. It expresses a metrical form of litany: ". . . the Falcon has destroyed the City of the Owl. The Two-Falcons has destroyed the City of the Palm. The Scorpion has destroyed the City of the Chapel. The Lion has destroyed the City of the Ka." It is perhaps the most telling document of the ultimate identity of language and representation in Egyptian art.

The King, Represented in Animal Forms,
Destroying Cities
Reverse of preceding palette.

THE VICTORY OF KING NARMER OVER
THE DELTA. *Circa 3100 B.C.*

The votive character of this work is underscored by its origin: it comes from Hierakonpolis, the sacred city of the prehistoric kingdom of Upper Egypt. The palette records the victory of King Narmer, who is shown once wearing the crown of Upper Egypt and again that of Lower Egypt. It is thus a monument commemorating the union, in the person of the King, of the two halves of Egypt, the "Two Lands" — after which the Nile Valley enters the age of history. King Narmer may perhaps be identified with King Menes, the legendary founder of the Egyptian dynasties.

The face of the palette (left), which has a hollow for grinding antimony, shows two heifers' heads — probably representing the goddess Hathor — between which appears the name of the King. Below, the sovereign — followed and preceded by high officials — advances behind four divine insignia that lead the way for him. Further along are ten decapitated enemies — identified by hieroglyphics — with their heads neatly set between their legs.

The strong desire to tell a story is apparent in the extensive series of elements and motifs. In identifying the figures by inscribing their names, and in the distinctive details of dress, the sculptor reveals that he had a specific event

The Victory of King Narmer Over the Delta
Early proto-dynastic period; circa 3100 B.C.
Carved schist; height 29 1/4″.
From Hierakonpolis. (3055)

in mind. Relating the size of the figures to their importance is a typically narrative device — almost a rhetorical element — to give the protagonist his due importance. In the lower register, the same theme is repeated in another vocabulary. The facts of the situation have been transformed into a system of general symbols: a bull (personifying the King) destroys a city wall with his horns and tramples an enemy under his hoof. An entirely different motif is seen in the central part of the palette. The long necks of two imaginary felines are interlaced around the central hollow. They are held on leashes by two symmetrically placed figures. The reduction of corresponding elements in the composition to a play of forms, and their fantastic deformation, are not part of Egyptian tradition but recall the art of Mesopotamia.

The narrative on the reverse of the palette (right) is conveyed in a gesture that sums up an entire event. In the group formed by the king — who is about to strike a blow — and the fallen enemy, there is an exact rendering of the event and at the same time a symbol (as shown by the hieroglyphic designation) of the vanquished. Similarly, the two fallen figures in the lower part are identified by two hieroglyphic signs (perhaps Memphis and Sais). Above on the right, a pictograph tells how Horus, the falcon god, brings in prisoners (symbolized by a head with marked ethnic features) from the swampy regions (indicated by swamp reeds). The loosely composed element of the dead enemies shown below and the cryptogram aspect of the detail of Horus make a counterpoint to the monumentality of the main group. Whatever serves in the narration is utilized without much concern for synchronizing the various modes of representation.

PORTRAIT STATUE OF KING ZOSER. *Dynasty III.* *p. 28*
King Zoser was the founder of classical Egypt, and his tomb, the Step Pyramid at Sakkara, is one of the greatest monuments of ancient Egypt. It is the summation of the architectural, representational and intellectual experience of Egypt at its beginnings. This statue comes from the tomb's *serdab,* a walled-off recess with vents giving onto the rooms in which the rites of the funerary cult took place. Out of sight itself, the statue could "see" through the little windows. A detail such as this shows the particular significance of archaic Egyptian sculpture, which was aimed at creating real entities, with their own autonomy, rather than objects for contemplation. This partiality for realism underscores the statue's function as a magic substitute for the person. It is peculiar to the archaic period, for in later centuries Egyptian artists did not retain this passionate faith in the "life" of a work of art. The desire to express life is seen here in the importance given to the head, with its heavy, intricate coiffure. The protuberant mouth and the eyes, originally of inlaid stone, must have added a touch of vivid naturalism. This descriptive and analytical ability is not reflected in the schematic monumental structure of the body seated on the throne (not shown here). It is a generalized mass treated merely as an element necessary to give prominence to the more expressive part of the statue.

THE MEMPHITE AGE

PRINCE RAHOTEP AND HIS CONSORT, PRINCESS NOFRET. *Dynasty IV.*

Little more than a century after the statue of Zoser, comes this statuary group representing one of the sons of an unnamed king (almost certainly Snefru) and his consort. Although they are carved out of two separate blocks, the statues were obviously meant to be seen together. Their excellent state of preservation provides valuable documentary evidence of the effects achieved by painting in Egyptian sculpture.

The "lifelike" intent of the statues has survived: it is said that the laborers who found them in 1871 fled in terror from the figures' glittering glances. Yet the artist's major concern is the rhythms within which the human body may be enclosed, and which define the function of each limb in the general structure. The faces are, accordingly, less characterized and less important than the economy of the whole. The rigor of the composition is carried by the framing elements: in contrast to Zoser's throne — in which the separate parts are shown — the chairs here have no naturalistic details. They are abstract cubes, and their backs serve in fact only to provide a frame for the figures. The figure of Nofret, completely wrapped in a mantle, may be compared with the cloaked figure of Zoser; in this later work, however, the mass of the body has been differentiated to show the articulation of the limbs and forms. An old technique has been used here as a point of departure for a new experiment in representation. This ability to graft new experiences onto tradition is the outstanding feature of Egyptian classicism.

Prince Rahotep and His Consort,
Princess Nofret
Beginning of Dynasty IV; circa 2600 B.C.
Painted limestone with inlaid eyes;
height 3′ 11″.
From the tomb of Rahotep at Medum.
(3, 4)

Above: detail.

31

BLACK DIORITE STATUE OF KING CHEPHREN. *Dynasty IV.*

King Chephren was the builder of the second pyramid of Giza. Even though some of the features of this statue are similar to those in others of Chephren, the theme here is the abstraction of royalty rather than the representation of a particular person. The royal spirit is seen in the impassive serenity of the face and in the fluent, assured pose. Here the right hand, holding a "plan," rests on the knee. In the older statue of Ráhotep (page 30), it is held against the breast, interrupting the clear development of the torso. Another royal element is seen in the symbols decorating the throne: the lions forming the legs and the emblematic and heraldic device of the "Union of the Two Lands" (represented by the papyrus and the lotus) on the sides. Finally, there is the figure of the falcon — representing the god Horus, the falcon god and archetype of the royal god who is incarnated in each successive sovereign — with wings spread at the back of the King's neck, placed there to protect him or perhaps to give him the breath of life by flapping its wings. These iconographic details are not extraneous to the composition, but provide a lateral view that completes and complements the frontal view of the work. Both views show the rhythmic geometric structure that regulates the relationships between the parts of the statue. The need to consider both sides constitutes an abstract way of creating a conceptual, three-dimensional framework for an impressive plastic vision. The material itself is the very hard stone, diorite, from a quarry in the Nubian desert, 625 miles from the place where it was used (as a sign of ownership, the name of the King was inscribed on a mass of the stone in the quarry). It recalls the use of another hard Egyptian stone, porphyry, in Roman imperial statuary of late classical times.

ALABASTER STATUE OF KING CHEPHREN. *Dynasty IV.*

A much less ambitious work than the preceding diorite statue of the King, this work has been ascribed by some scholars to a late period with an archaizing taste. This is certainly a mistaken view, but it stresses the fact that there was a broad range of expression during the Fourth Dynasty. Here the volumetric composition and the relationships between the various parts of the body are simpler and more explicit, from the cubic seat to the simplification of the musculature. It is precisely this quality, which states a theme that is not so successfully developed as in the preceding statue, that makes it a less important piece.

32

Alabaster Statue of King Chephren
Dynasty IV; circa 2558–2533 B.C.
Alabaster with traces of
polychromy; height 30 1/4".
From Memphis (?). (41)

Black Diorite Statue of King Chephren
Dynasty IV; circa 2558–2533 B.C.
Black diorite veined with white;
height 5′ 6″.
From the temple near the King's pyramid
at Giza. (14)

34

KING MYCERINUS BETWEEN THE GODDESS HATHOR AND THE GODDESS OF DIOSPOLIS PARVA. *Dynasty IV*.

A series of related monuments from the funerary works dedicated to King Mycerinus, the builder of the third great pyramid of Giza, were intended to celebrate the monarch's sovereignty over all of Egypt. Four of them have survived. They show Mycerinus flanked by the goddess Hathor (with heifers' horns and solar disk in her role of celestial diety) and by personifications of different provinces.

This work shows the typical features of Memphite art — in the clear definition of relationships, the rigorous rhythm, and the framing element of the background slab. The curves of the goddesses' breasts, the crowns and the faces are executed with feeling and restraint. The tradition represented by the diorite statue of Chephren (page 33) — rigorously developed form without stereotyped devices — is serenely maintained here. To some extent it is a point of departure, for the most specific theme of this period is the construction of "groups" of figures of the same size. Compared to the relationship between the statues of Rahotep and Nofret (page 30), the rhythm between the two female figures and the male advancing from the background in the center is more complex. The concept is still simple, but the lessons learned in representing the single standing figure have been applied to create more intricate spatial relationships.

RESERVE HEAD. *Dynasty IV*. *p. 36*

In some of the family tombs of Cheops and Chephren, a "reserve head," instead of a funerary statue, was placed in the coffin chamber. These heads typically have a flat base, so that in the course of the rites they could be placed on the ground. The heads are made of unpainted limestone and often have intentionally broken ears and a rough incision scratched on the top of the skull. The hair is close-fitting and cap-like. About twenty such works are known, and they appear to be evidence of a funerary ritual that later went out of use.

Aside from religious custom, this series is significant for the light it casts on portraiture during Egyptian art's most formal period. Each head has its identifying features. Often there is only one such element, the most typical for identification of a person — just as in the most ancient biographies a single, salient fact is recorded to sum up an entire life. The portrait, like the biography, is only a means of identifying a person in order to guarantee his survival. This practical interest in supplying a surrogate for the body is akin to the use of stucco funerary masks immortalizing the features of the dead, which are also known in this period. The fundamental difference, however, is that it is expressed in the works of the royal stone carvers in

King Mycerinus Between the Goddess Hathor and the Goddess of Diospolis Parva
Dynasty IV; circa 2510 B.C.
Dark schist with traces of polychromy; height 33″.
From the temple near the King's pyramid at Giza. (46499)

Reserve Head
Dynasty IV; circa 2550 B.C.
White limestone; height 7 1/2".
From the necropolis at Giza. (46216)

terms of the strictest Memphite geometrical composition. In this fusion of abstract form and specific physiognomy lies the attraction of the heads.

PORTRAIT OF KING USERKAF. *Dynasty V.*

The taste for simplified geometric form was the conscious expression of the rationalistic bent of Fourth Dynasty art. Successive periods carried on this austere heritage, and it remained an important and distinctive part of the Egyptian figurative vocabulary. Here we have a classically austere example of royal sculpture. Everything is reduced to a few essentials, and the effect of this process is heightened by the unusual size of the figure. With the exception of the Sphinx, this is the earliest example of a colossal statue. The sober grandeur of the genre reminds us of the significance of the Memphite vision of art.

Portrait of King Userkaf
Dynasty V; 2494–2337 B.C.
Pink granite; height 26".
From the temple of the King's pyramid
at Sakkara. (52501)

"THE SHEIK EL BELED." *Dynasty V.*

Although the official represented here was a certain Kaaper, the statue reminded the workers who discovered it in 1860 of the mayor of their village, and the statue has since been known by his title. Carved in wood, the figure is more freely developed than similar works in stone. In the latter, both arms are pressed close to the body, in the classical pose of the Egyptian nobility: the left hand raised to grasp a staff resting on the ground, the right hand holding a scepter at a right angle to the body. Here the composition is not only three-dimensional, but also spatial. (The place for lodging the scepter is evident, but the object is missing.) The desire to create a realistic identity is seen in the spherical forms of the head and the slightly bulging belly. This balance between interest in style and interest in reality is rarely surpassed in Egyptian sculpture.

PORTRAIT OF A PERSONAGE. *Dynasty V.*

This statue of an anonymous official, from Sakkara, may be another representation of Kaaper; this suggests the interesting prospect that works entirely different in character may have been commissioned by the same subject. Compared to the absolute novelty of "The Sheik el Beled," this carefully carved figure has a highly decorous but insipid grace, bordering on sentimentality. Here the rules of Memphite "cubism" have been applied methodically and without invention.

"THE WIFE OF THE SHEIK EL BELED." *Dynasty V.*

This statue was also found in the tomb of Kaaper, and thus probably merits the nickname that is generally given to it. The most obvious divergence in technique from the statues of the subject's husband is seen in the eyes, which are incised in the wood (and consequently were only painted) rather than inlaid. The wig is similar to that of Nofret (page 30), but stands away from the shoulders, making the figure lighter and livelier. The rhythmic development of the volumes is much simpler, and there is a straightforward approach that foreshadows the final phases of Memphite art.

STATUE OF RANOFER, PROPHET OF
PTAH AND SOKARI. *Dynasty V.*   *pp. 40–41*

This statue of the priest of the god Ptah, the patron of artisans, is certainly the work of one of the best official sculptors of the Memphite period. With this statue (and the following one), the theme of the male body entered the official repertory. It is probably the interpretation, in compact form,

Left:
"The Sheik el Beled"
Beginning of Dynasty V;
twenty-fifth century B.C.
Sycamore wood and inlaid eyes (legs and
cane have been restored); height 3′ 7″.
From Sakkara. (34)

Above:
Portrait of a Personage
Beginning of Dynasty V.
Sycamore wood with traces of colored
plaster and inlaid eyes; height 27″.
From Sakkara. (32)

Above, right:
"The Wife of the Sheik el Beled"
Beginning of Dynasty V.
Wood; height 24″.
From Sakkara. (33)

of an observed pose in real life — one arm is extended to grasp a staff and the other hangs down along the body, the hand holding a scepter. Here, however, the too obviously illustrative attributes have been eliminated, leaving only the grip of the closed hands. Instead of one arm coming forward, both are held close to the body, thus closing the composition. The forward foot is solidly attached to the background slab, making the statue appear more stable. The robust, static quality of the composition, and the existence of a background slab, confirm that the statue was meant to be seen as standing still, not walking.

The simplicity and traditional aspects of the composition reveal the liveliness of the artist's inspiration. The surfaces are carefully and lovingly modeled in relation to the simplified but live musculature, which sets the rhythm for the whole composition and enriches it with a play of light and dark. The head in particular, coming forward from the background slab with striking effect, shows the importance of the play of light in the composition. Shadow lies deep under the wig, which is not so much a frame for the face as a means of making it stand out from the shade. The detail of the face on page 41 reveals the delicate play of the surface planes (the nose has been restored).

Statue of Ranofer, Prophet of
Ptah and Sokari
Dynasty V.
Painted limestone; height 5' 11".
From Ranofer's tomb at Sakkara. (18)

Right: detail.

PORTRAIT STATUE OF RANOFER, PROPHET OF PTAH AND SOKARI. *Dynasty V.*

This second statue of Ranofer is related to the preceding one, as are the two statues of Kaaper to each other. The first statue of Ranofer has a close-fitting wig, wears a narrowly pleated kilt and is athletically built; this one has no wig, its kilt is longer and the body heavier. The existence of two different types of statues of the same subject has been interpreted as a means of showing the owner of the tomb at two different periods of his life (in youth and old age or in official and private life). This use of two statues probably provided the precedent for the curious custom of representing the deceased in a group of two or three statues seated together, as at a family gathering.

An interesting experiment was carried out on this wigless figure of Ranofer: a cast of the wig on the other statue was placed on its head, revealing the very close resemblance between the two. This is not enough, however, to justify considering them portraits, but it does indicate that the two statues are from the same workshop and by the same master — at least in the parts requiring the most skill.

Left:
Portrait Statue of Ranofer,
Prophet of Ptah and Sokari
Dynasty V.
Painted limestone; height 5′ 11″.
From Ranofer's tomb at Sakkara. (19)

Above, right:
Portrait Statue of Ti
End of Dynasty V; twenty-fourth
century B.C.
Painted limestone; height 6′ 5″.
From the tomb of Ti at Sakkara. (20)

Right: detail.

PORTRAIT STATUE OF TI. *Dynasty V.*

Ti's was one of the most famous tombs of the Memphite age, decorated richly and with great variety. This statue from its funerary cult chamber is one of the most notable monuments of the end of the Fourth Dynasty. The similarity in type to the two preceding statues is apparent, but here the tendency to follow a formula has become dominant and there is an explicit and facile compliance with the geometrical scheme of the composition. The prominence given to the triangular apron and the sketchy rendering of anatomical form also indicate a decline in quality from the Fourth Dynasty. **43**

Statue of an Unknown Personage
Dynasty V; twenty-fifth — twenty-fourth
century B.C.
Painted limestone with inlaid eyes;
height 24".
From Sakkara. (35)

STATUE OF AN UNKNOWN PERSONAGE. *Dynasty V.*

The anonymous subject is posed in accordance with a scheme from Fourth-Dynasty sculpture, which was of interest to the sculptor mainly as a framework on which to exercise his technique. An uncommon feature, however, is the detaching of the arms from the body — an attempt to set the statue in air as well as in space. Another notable element is the spirited expression of the face, which appears to be on the point of smiling. In a work that is otherwise not outstanding in quality, these features foreshadow new requirements in art.

STATUE OF AN UNKNOWN SCRIBE. *Dynasty V.* *p. 46*

The theme of the scribe, as a representation of the owner of the tomb, originated in Fourth-Dynasty princely circles. Some fifty examples from the Memphite age are known. Hard stone, such as granite and diorite, was often used for these highly valued works. The quality of the workmanship is consistently high, indicating that the theme was considered unusually noble. Egyptian civilization depended more on administrators than on warriors, so that showing the deceased as a man of letters was a true honor. Activity in sculpture makes its appearance in these statues for the first time in the historic period. Limitless and motionless time was implied in earlier Egyptian sculpture. Here, time is dynamic, with an immediate future potential: by holding an inkwell in his hand, the subject shows that he is ready to act. More than an external iconographic motif that can be added to the subject, this is the beginning of a new conception of representation. In this statue, the interest in the dynamic and the unique extends from the type and composition of the figure to the expression of the face. A psychological character and a specific moment are identified by means of a play of plastic effects in which there is no formalistic complacency. The wig provides a transition to the shoulders; in the statue of Ranofer (page 40), it creates the shadow that throws the face into greater relief. The composition here is the traditional one for this type. What is not traditional is the detaching of the hands from the body and the energetic position of the fingers of the right hand. These are lively, realistic and narrative elements that give the composition force and convey its charge of vitality.

This statue forms a pair with the preceding *Statue of an Unknown Personage*. Both were found in the same tomb; yet this one is full of personality, while the other has a certain banality.

THE KNEELING SCRIBE. *Dynasty V.* *p. 47*

Traditionally known as *The Kneeling Scribe,* this statue in fact portrays the funerary priest Ka-em-ked. It was found in the tomb of an illustrious Fifth Dynasty prince, Ur-irni, with other statuettes of attendants. This is a new category of sculpture, since it represents a public servant. The pose is also

new: kneeling, the priest humbly folds his hands and looks toward his master. The fine workmanship (the eyes are inlaid) and the evident psychological interest in the devotedly obedient expression enhance the novelty of applying the rules of Memphite volumetrics to new compositions of the human figure.

WOMAN GRINDING GRAIN. *Dynasty V.*   *p. 48*
This statuette of a servant named Ishat comes from the same tomb as the preceding work. It is one of the figurines, common in this period, that supplemented the tomb's wall decorations and illustrated the activities that provide offerings for the deceased in the afterlife. These little statues of

Woman Grinding Grain
Dynasty V; twenty-fourth century B.C.
Painted limestone; height 11″.
From Sakkara. (110)

servants are often crudely executed in wood. In minor tombs they took the place of wall paintings, which required the extensive wall surfaces only found in the more important burials.

The principal feature of these figures is that they "accomplish" an action; that is, they are seen in a narrative and dynamic, rather than a static and descriptive, function. In this respect they embody a popular feeling and reflect an attitude that was current in archaic times, when statues much more frequently represented some activity (the dancing women of the predynastic period, for example). This contact with daily life and a certain freedom of form in expressing it indicate the formation of a new taste, although no new attitude is apparent in the more official art of the period.

SERVANT WASHING A JAR.   *Dynasty V*.

The activity this figure is engaged in lent itself to the creation of a completely new composition, with the forward movement of the knees naturally enclosing the space in which the hands are shown working around the jar. In the ease with which the descriptive effect has been achieved,

48

Above, left:
Servant Washing a Jar
Dynasty V.
Painted limestone; height 13″.
From Sakkara. (112)

there appears to be none of the traditional, careful Memphite calculations; however, these have in fact been perfectly assimilated in the construction of the work. But other sources of experience are suggested by the three hollows in the front of the base, where three vases must have been set to complete the jar-washing scene. These objects, which could be put into or taken out of the composition, are certainly not part of the sculptural tradition. In conception they are connected with contemporary narrative wall paintings, whose inspiration influenced not only the type but also the interest in story telling in this "minor" sculpture.

THE BREWER. *Dynasty V.*

Above, right:
The Brewer
Dynasty V.
Painted limestone; height 16″
From Sakkara. (117)

Egyptian beer was made by fermenting lightly baked barley cakes that were soaked in water. The liquid was then filtered and stored in pitchers. It was served on every table, even the poorest, for beer was the national drink. This statuette represents a servant filtering the soaked barley mash through a sieve. The position of the arms and the stance, which are required by the activity, create an unusual rhythmic composition.

STATUE OF THE FUTURE KING PEPI II (?). *Dynasty VI.*

This small copper statue, representing a child, has importance in the history of technology. Metal statues on this scale are unknown in later Egyptian history, since the intrinsic value of the material made it likely that they would be melted down. The statue appears to be made up of sheets of copper molded into shape by hammering and then nailed to a wooden core. Only the face seems to have been cast. The work, with its larger companion statute, comes from a temple, not a tomb. The statues were originally highly polished and inlaid with gilded stucco and perhaps with lapis lazuli. In composition, the figures belong to an older tradition, but the sumptuous effect of the high finish and precious materials give them a new sensuous aura.

Statue of the Future King Pepi II (?)
Dynasty VI; circa 2310 B.C.
Hammered copper; height 24″.
From Kom el Ahmar. (33035)

STATUE OF THE COURT PHYSICIAN NY-ANK-RA.
Dynasty VI.

It has been suggested that this statue represents a cripple, or that it shows a person in the act of sitting down and adjusting his kilt with his hands. What is important in the composition, however, is the rejection of static regularity. A balance is sought with respect to the central axis, which gives a new, though somewhat elementary, content to the representation. The structure of the body and the head are both uninspired and traditional.

PORTRAIT OF THE DWARF KHNUMHOTEP. *Dynasty VI.*

Much more vital and divorced from tradition than the preceding work is this figure of an "Overseer of the Funerary Priests' Vestments." He is dressed in a long kilt, wears no wig; his hands are open and his feet aligned (instead of the traditional pose with hands making fists and the left foot forward). These variations from the norm are in tune with the disproportion of the body, the thick squat limbs, the distended belly, and the "speaking" expression of the face. All these elements reflect a taste for description and anecdote that goes beyond Memphite classicism. Yet these vital features make a counterpoint with the "cubist" vocabulary of Memphite composition, and precious effects are avoided in favor of a subdued contemplative atmosphere.

Statue of the Court Physician Ny-ank-Ra
Beginning of Dynasty VI;
twenty-third century B.C.
Painted limestone; height 25".
From the necropolis at Giza. (Giza 49)

Portrait of the Dwarf Khnumhotep
Beginning of Dynasty VI;
twenty-fourth century B.C.
Painted limestone; height 18".
From Sakkara. (144)

Portrait Statue of Ur-khuui
Fragment.
Dynasty VI (?); twenty-third century B.C.
Limestone with traces of color; height 14".

PORTRAIT STATUE OF UR-KHUUI. *Dynasty VI.*

The rough technique used in this statue, probably a work of the Sixth Dynasty, illustrates an interest in the unusual and the immediately expressive. The eyes are small, the mouth slants, the face is plain, and the cap of hair frames an irregular brow. Canonical athletic musculature has been replaced in what remains of the body by sagging folds of flesh. All these features show that a drive to expression has found its outlet within the terms of a standardized type of sculpture.

THE DWARF SENEB AND HIS FAMILY. *Dynasty VI.*

This tiny group was placed in a hollowed-out block of stone — set in a wall — that was closed with a facing stone with two peepholes in it. There was also an offering to the statues in a number of little alabaster vases. Seneb was an important official, head of the royal textile works, with many titles; his wife was entitled to be called princess.

Unassuming though it is, this work is one of the most revolutionary of the period. Within the rigid geometrical Memphite framework, it expresses a

The Dwarf Seneb and His Family
Dynasty VI; twenty-third century B.C.
Painted limestone; height 13".
From Seneb's tomb at Giza. (51281)

Portrait of the Court Official Hesira
Dynasty III; twenty-seventh century B.C.,
around the time of Zoser.
Height 3′ 9″.
From Hesira's tomb at Sakkara. (1427)

whole new line of experiment and aspiration. The axis of the composition divides the work into two equivalent but different halves, with the woman on the right and the man and the children on the left. Equivalent rhythm takes the place of symmetry. On the horizontal axis, similarly, the cadence of the two torsos above is not completed below in the expected way. Instead there is the surprise of the two figures of the children in place of the man's legs. Similar dynamic elements also appear in the separate figures. The inadequate arms and legs and the large expressive head of the dwarf are alien to the established tradition of representing fine bodies. Even more, the directness and the costume of the woman, which at first seem to recall Nofret (page 30), are in effect a mocking vernacular translation of that figure. The movement of the head and body off the vertical suggest a warm familial relationship with the husband that is very far from the impersonal calm of earlier Memphite sculpture. Expression and narrative intention radiate from every detail and justify a certain slackness in the execution. The sculptor's technique is no longer tied to the refined calculations of the original conception of Memphite plastic art.

PORTRAIT OF THE COURT OFFICIAL HESIRA. *Dynasty III.*
Eleven wooden panels lined the backs of the niches in the wall of sun-dried bricks in the tomb of Hesira at Sakkara. Their dating is established by the name of King Zoser on seals found in the excavation, as well as by the archaic character of the building. Two of these panels are virtually intact. In the one shown here, we see the beginning of the classical tradition in Egypt. It is immediately apparent in the arrangement of the hair and the kilt — which will remain constant for centuries — and in the symbolic and elegant construction of the figure, seen partly full face and partly in profile. The relationship between the various parts is limpidly expressed, for they are analyzed and composed without being forced into a rigid symmetrical system. The text and the representation are clearly distinguished in the panel, so that there is no confusion of interest. Although the hieroglyphics are drawn very carefully, they all have the abstract but not mechanical elegance of a page of print. In the representational part the composition is just as refined. There is no real stress on the central division, yet the vertical axis determines the dynamic balance between the figure on the left and the empty space on the right. The space is not bleakly empty, for standing out in it are the attributes of the official's rank: the scepter, and the scribe's equipment of pen, palette and inkwells. This allusion to compositional schemes that are not automatically fully developed is seen also in the system of orthogonals between elements that are almost horizontal and elements that are almost vertical. Thus the surface movements created by the anatomical notations describe the spaces and rhythms of the figuration. In this work Egyptian art leaves behind the eloquent but often arid vocabulary of predynastic relief, and establishes the detached and self-sufficient rigor of form on which later tradition will be built, whether in agreement or in opposition.

PAINTING OF GEESE FROM MEDUM. *Dynasty IV*.

This panel is part of a much larger composition and was meant to be seen in counterpoint with a series of other elements. A typical feature of Egyptian painting, however, is the juxtaposition of highly autonomous sequences, so that one can view this panel as an independent work of art. The clear, simple composition comes close to mirror symmetry. This arrangement reflects a common way of constructing groups in a dynamic "two plus one" rhythm. The lively color is a vital element, as it redeems the schematic composition of the work. The importance given to the extensive neutral ground, against which the figures of the geese are shown, is typical of the most ancient manner of painting (which will be revived and exaggerated later as a consciously archaizing motif).

PORTRAIT OF KA-EM-HESET, CHIEF OF THE MASONS. *Dynasty V*.

This panel must have had a use similar to that of Hesira (page 54); it also belonged to the decoration of a tomb at Sakkara. Comparison with its prototype reveals how quickly the original stylistic conception became dry journeyman's work. To remain valid, such a conception has to be continually nourished by direct experience; this is not the case in this simple representation of a figure. It occurs only in the complex scenes that cover the walls of contemporary temples and tombs.

SLAB PORTRAYING RA-UR. *Dynasty V*. p. 58

This work shows hedonistic virtuosity in the use of a precious material, alabaster, as part of a wall. Above the face, with its lightly modeled planes, are heavily incised hieroglyphics. Below, the body is outlined by firmly drawn contours. The sophistication of the execution properly complements the special luminous quality of the alabaster.

Painting of Geese From Medum
Beginning of Dynasty IV; twenty-seventh century B.C.
Tempera on plaster; width 5′ 8″.
From the tomb of Itat at Medum. (1742)

Portrait of Ka-em-heset,
Chief of the Masons
Dynasty V; twenty-fourth century B.C.
Inlaid relief on wood;
height of the figure 3′ 1″.
From Ka-em-heset's at Sakkara.

57

58

Slab Portraying Ra-ur
Dynasty V; twenty-fifth — twenty-fourth
century B.C.
Alabaster with traces of color.
From Ra-ur's tomb at Giza. (6267)

SARCOPHAGUS OF RA-UR. *Dynasty V.*
The Memphite stone coffins often depend for their effect on simplicity of
form and perfect cutting. In this example there is also an interesting play
of details that recall the floral decoration used on house facades. The details emphasize the coffin's function as the "house of the dead," and enliven
the surface with a finely executed play of light and line.

DANCERS, HARPIST AND SINGERS. *Dynasty V.*

This detail of a wall painting shows a harpist and two singers (above), and two dancers and two women clapping hands as they sing (below). The complete scene has a number of additional figures in similar attitudes, with the same flat rendering and the same spacing. The inscriptions provide generic titles: "Singing," "Playing the Harp," "Dancing." We have here the first development of Egyptian relief painting, which was used on a large scale in the decoration of temples and tombs. It shows an increasingly explicit interest in broad scenes of action and narration. This amplitude calls for an organization of the narrative that is, in effect, the organization of the surfaces to be decorated. Thus the space is divided into a system of successive layers. The musicians and the dancers are obviously to be imagined as together, but they have been placed in separate registers so that all the features of each figure are shown. The detailed description is made even more explicit by the accompanying written commentary.

Dancers, Harpist and Singers
Detail.
Dynasty V; twenty-fourth century B.C.
Stuccoed and painted limestone relief; width 5′ 1″.
From the tomb of Ny-kheft-Ka.
From Sakkara. (1533)

FIGHT AMONG BOATMEN. *Dynasty V.*

A comparison of the Hesira relief (page 54), the preceding relief and this present work illuminates the history of two-dimensional representation in the Memphite age. In the Hesira relief, the portrayal was stripped of every active element, with the vitality of the figure expressed by a play of dynamic balances. A static perfection was the consequence. In the relief on page 60, narrative was the determining factor in the composition, leading to a rational distribution, in preordained cadences, of the elements. Activity was expressed by the repetition of the same actions, creating a foreseeable rhythm. In this example, what motivates the renewal of established compositional schemes is the desire to tell an adventurous and dramatic, rather than a composed and predictable, story. The crews of the two boats are fighting. A sailor has fallen into the water and one of his mates is pulling him out by his heels. The bodies are intertwined or placed in opposition; their gestures are more frenetic than violent. The inscription in the upper part of the scene includes the cry of one of the combatants: "His back is broken!"

Fight Among Boatmen
Dynasty VI; twenty-third century B.C.
Stuccoed and painted limestone relief;
width 4′ 9″.
From Sakkara. (1535)

This work marks a revival of the popular taste for vivid reality and narrative that had been eclipsed by the revolution in form which created the staid courtly art of the early Memphite age. Yet this plunge into the liveli-

ness of daily reality is not empiric and instinctive realism. In the tangle of boatmen, classical compositional schemes, such as the "two plus one," are still to be seen. This ability to renew stylistic form by changing the meaning of stylistics is typical of Egyptian art.

GOLDEN HAWK OF HIERAKONPOLIS. *Dynasty VI.*

This fragment of a sacred hawk is from Hierakonpolis, the city that was sacred to the hawk god. The headdress identifies the hawk as a god, for the circlet is surmounted by two stylized vertical feathers (a typical emblem of the celestial gods of Upper Egypt) and in front has the uraeus, or the cobra protector of the sun gods and their kinsmen on earth, the kings. The body of the hawk was discovered during the excavation which uncovered the head, but it was lost during the course of the digging. It was made of copper and had the strong stylization typical of sacred images. It may have had in front of it the figure of a sovereign, who would have been the donor shown under the protection of the god.

The two parts of the statue, in gold and in bronze, were fastened together with countersunk rivets. The head was hammered into shape and finished with a chisel. The eyes are the ends of bars of obsidian. This is the most elaborate surviving example of Memphite goldsmith's work, and is perfectly in keeping with the sculptural canons of the time.

Golden Hawk of Hierakonpolis
Fragment of a cult statue.
Dynasty VI; circa twenty-second century B.C.
Cut and hammered sheet gold, with inlaid eyes; height 14″.
From the temple of Hierakonpolis. (52701)

THE MIDDLE KINGDOM

Woman Bearing Offerings
Dynasty XI; twenty-first century B.C.
Stuccoed and painted wood; height
(without base) 4′ 1″.
From Dier el Bahari. (46725)

Soldiers
Dynasty IX-X; twenty-second
century B.C.
Painted wood;
length of the base 6′ 4″.
From Asyut. (258)

WOMAN BEARING OFFERINGS. *Dynasty XI.*

This statuette of a servant, from an Eleventh Dynasty tomb, recalls various examples of similar subjects from the Memphite age. The freedom of movement that can be rendered in wood is shown here by the naturalness of the arm supporting the basket on the head. The pointed ends of four loaves of bread stick up out of the basket. This realistic detail draws the eye and, in fact, the whole composition builds upward, creating a dynamic and tentative balance.

SOLDIERS. *Dynasty IX–X.*

Military themes were very common early in the Middle Kingdom. Forty soldiers armed with bronze-tipped spears and shields are shown here marching four abreast. Another similar group from the same tomb is made up of forty archers. The taste for models and miniature groups originated in the late Memphite age. Here it is fully developed, although there is not yet a complete grasp of how a representational composition, originally conceived as pictorial, should be extended in space.

PRESENTATION OF THE CATTLE. *Dynasty XI.*

A series of small figures in wood comes from the tomb of Meket Ra at Deir el Bahari, which was built close to the tombs of the kings Mentuhotep I, II and III, all of whom he served as a high official. The practical reason that inspired these works was the same as that of the statuettes of servants, but here the results are much more elaborate. Scenes of this type were intended to show how rich the occupant of the tomb was, and how his wealth procured him offerings even after his death. This scene — crowded with men and animals — is obviously taken from pictorial models. But what was simply a problem of representation on a flat surface in wall paintings has become a sort of stage model here. The separate elements are unimportant in themselves and, in fact, the execution of the figures is careless. The artist was clearly more interested in the general composition. In the reality of the small, confined space the figures — seen from the back, in profile or overlapping one another — resolve the motifs that had to be carefully detailed for the spectator in two-dimensional representations. The spectator has to move if he wants to take in the details. The space of the sculptural work is the same as that in which the observer functions. This new sense of organic space, which liberates the work of art from its purely rational position in Memphite geometric space, was a necessary prelude to the Middle Kingdom conception of mass as an organic quantity.

Presentation of the Cattle
Dynasty XI; twenty-first century B.C.
Painted wood; length of the base 5' 9".
From Deir el Bahari (Thebes). (46724)

STATUE OF KING NEB-KETEP-RA MENTUHOTEP IN THE COSTUME OF APOTHEOSIS. *Dynasty XI.*

The statue comes from the monumental mortuary temple built by the king at Deir el Bahari. It is one of a group of eight seated and standing statues

*Statue of King Neb-hetep-Ra Mentuhotep
in the Costume of Apotheosis*
Dynasty XI; 2060–2010 B.C.
Painted gray sandstone; height 5' 9".
From the king's mortuary temple at
Deir el Bahari. (36195)

that was placed in the garden in front of the monument, and which showed the sovereign in the short cloak typical of the costume of apotheosis (*sed*). This work, however, had a different function from that of the others in the group. It was wrapped in bandages like a mummy and placed in a funerary niche in the monument, almost as if it were a substitute for the real body of the king. Its perfect state of preservation allows an exact evaluation of the execution, including the elementary color scheme which sets the particular tone of the work. We see that here the debased Memphite representational devices of provincial art following the Sixth Dynasty became the point of departure for a new interpretation of the same schemes. The heaviness of the forms, the elementary execution and the indifference to any play of dynamic balances go to make up a massive figure, which is aggressive in its gravity and barbarous in its authority.

STATUETTE OF SESOSTRIS I WEARING THE WHITE CROWN. *Dynasty XII.*

This statuette, wearing the crown of Upper Egypt, formed a pair with a similar piece wearing the crown of Lower Egypt, which is now in the Metropolitan Museum of Art in New York. Both figures probably were used in the funeral ceremonies of a vizier of the king, from whose mortuary monument they come. The artist was inspired by the fluid modeling and the separation of the limbs from the trunk that are seen in the wood statuettes of the Memphite age. A degree of facial characterization derives from the same Memphite tradition; in fact, the work comes from the region of Memphis.

STATUE OF SESOSTRIS I. *Dynasty XII.*

This statue is one of a series of ten similar statues placed so as to encircle anyone entering the funerary chapel of the tomb of Sesostris I. It shows close study and analysis, in the relationship between the feet and the plane on which they rest, and between the hands and the thighs. At the same time the entire figure is harmoniously and serenely unified. The appeal here to Memphite tradition is ultimately a Neoclassical intention with a political coloring. The reaffirmation of that tradition implicitly meant a restatement of royal continuity, in contrast to the deviations of the feudal age, of which the statute of Mentuhotep (page 67) is an example. The use of a number of similar figures created an obsessive image of regality, thus exploiting entirely different effects from those at which the separate works seem to be aiming. It is this that gives additional significance to a monument which at first seems to be coldly academic.

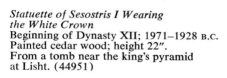

*Statuette of Sesostris I Wearing
the White Crown*
Beginning of Dynasty XII; 1971–1928 B.C.
Painted cedar wood; height 22″.
From a tomb near the king's pyramid
at Lisht. (44951)

Statue of Sesostris I
Dynasty XII; 1971–1928 B.C.
White limestone; height 6′ 5″.
From the king's mortuary temple
at Lisht. (411)

HEAD OF A WOMAN WITH SEPARATE WIG. *Dynasty XII.*

A wooden wig, painted black with gold decorations, was added to this small head. Such removable wigs, which appear on other statues of the period, were perhaps designed to allow for changes of coiffure. Similarly fluent, graceful feminine faces can be seen in statues carved in stone, such as the granite statues of the wife of the official Hapi-gefa from Kerma, in Boston. The artists' concern was a refined means of expressing organic vitality. A comparison with the head of Nefert (page 71) reveals the difference between the abstract form of that work and the interest in organic structure of this one.

QUEEN NEFERT, CONSORT OF SESOSTRIS II. *Dynasty XII.*

This is one of two similar statues of Queen Nefert. Both are in black granite and show a remarkable virtuosity in working with this rather intractable material. Originally the eyes were inlaid. In composition this figure is quite conventional, and is obviously modeled on statues of men.

Head of a Woman With Separate Wig
Beginning of Dynasty XII;
twentieth century B.C.
Wood with traces of color; the eyes must
have been inlaid.
From a tomb near the pyramid of
Sesostris I at Lisht.

Its novelty, however, lies in the coiffure; it is arranged in the "Hathoric" style, frequently used in images of the goddess Hathor, and thus alludes to the identification of the queen with the goddess. The coiffure, with its flexible turns and coils, enlivens the face. It is much more complex in its spiraling and swelling rhythms than the traditional Egyptian wigs.

CUBE STATUE OF HETEP THE TREASURER. *Dynasty XII.*

p. 72

This statue, with a similar work in limestone, is from a tomb in which a certain amount of Sixth Dynasty material was reused in a revival of Memphite architectural motifs. It has been suggested that the figure's curious pose is a sculptural interpretation of a well-known Old Kingdom theme: that of a figure seated in a litter with sides and back like those of the stone block. An iconographical origin of this sort would require a conscious desire to return to an archaic form. In fact, however, the theme is completely new and belongs to the group of so-called cube statues, the first examples of which appear at this time. The bodies of these statues are reduced to a single geometrical mass, similar to the one shown here — but with no anatomical details, since the clothes cover the entire figure, revealing only the folded hands and the feet. The head takes on special prominence, forming a smaller block upon the larger block of the body. This example is more complicated than other instances of radical cubistic sim-

Queen Nefert, Consort of Sesostris II
Dynasty XII; 1897–1878 B.C.
Black granite; height 5′ 5″.
From Tanis. (382)

Cube Statue of Hetep the Treasurer
Middle of Dynasty XII; nineteenth
century B.C.
Dark granite; height 29".
From the chapel in the masteba of Hetep,
the treasurer at Sakkara. (48858)

plification. Here we have an interpenetration of the geometric cube with anatomical forms. The various parts are enlivened and given an organic quality through the definition of muscles and ligaments. This curious counterpoint of the geometric and the organic, with both determining the sculptural mass, gives the work its singular character.

HEAD OF SESOSTRIS III. *Dynasty XII.*

Sesostris III was almost certainly the model for this head. The identification is borne out by the facial features and the manner of execution, as well as by the fact that the head was found in a temple he built. The talent for portraiture in ancient works of Egyptian art is again apparent in this head, which expresses more complex themes than did the earlier examples. In the early works, one or more typical features of a person were translated into clear geometrical and logical forms, occasionally attaining the perfect balance between characterization and absoluteness that is found in the *Sheik el Beled* (page 38). But references to an individual are to some

Head of Sesostris III
Dynasty XII; 1878–1843 B.C.
Black granite; height 11".
From the temple of Medamud. (486)

extent opposed to the typological generalization of archaic art, which reflects a society in which individual facts have value only to the extent that they corroborate an established, canonical order. In provincial art there is an inability to take on the complexities of Memphite rationalism, and an amiable tendency to see things as they are rather than as they should be. This is an archaic attitude, but in the crisis of Memphite art it became a conscious sense of the richness of nature and the legitimacy of exploring individual cases.

In literature of the period, general maxims were replaced by tales of particular situations and by true narratives. So in representation, rational idealization of form gave way to the search for the organic structures that in each case determine the form. Thus this portrait represents the completed process of the pursuit of an organic whole we have seen in various other works of this period.

Sphinx of Amenemhet III
Dynasty XII; 1842–1797 B.C.
Black granite; length 7′ 5″.
From Tanis. (394)

SPHINX OF AMENEMHET III. *Dynasty XII.*

A group of four sphinxes from Tanis shows an iconographical peculiarity: the royal head is framed by a lion's mane rather than a regal headdress. Since their discovery in 1860, this detail and the execution of the faces — found only in monuments from Tanis — suggested barbarian influence. Tanis may have been the capital of the kingdom set up by the Hyksos invaders, so these statues, including the group of sphinxes, were called "Hyksos monuments." The faces of the sphinxes, however, were identified in 1893 as representing Amenemhet III, through comparison with securely attributed portrait statues of that pharaoh. The numerous inscriptions of other sovereigns on these monuments merely represent various usurpations.

The example reproduced here has the best preserved face (despite the unfelicitously restored ears) and conveys the exceptional significance of these works. The potential power of the animal at rest and the personality of the sovereign's face derive their vitality from the skillful interpretation of their organic structures in the composition of the masses. At the same time they are carefully developed in terms of surface movements, thus utilizing the play of light as a means of expression, which is one of the great discoveries of Middle Kingdom art.

AMENEMHET III IN PRIESTLY COSTUME. *Dynasty XII.*

Although this highly unusual monument is ascribed to Amenemhet, his name does not actually appear on the work. He is shown in this fragment in striking priestly vestments, wearing a heavy wig, a leopard skin on his shoulders, various necklaces, and two insignia crowned with hawks' heads. There are no comparable statues combining this assortment of attributes. The same taste for unusual iconography seen in the sphinx from Tanis and

Amenemhet III in Priestly Costume
Fragment.
Dynasty XII; 1842–1797 B.C.
Black granite; height 3′ 3″.
From Mit Fares (Fayum). (395)

Two Male Figures Bearing River Offerings
Dynasty XII; 1842–1797 B.C.
Gray granite; height 5′ 3″.
From Tanis. (392)

Portrait of Amenemhet III
Dynasty XII; 1842–1797 B.C.
Yellowish limestone; height 5′ 3″.
From Hawwara (Fayum). (385)

in the piece on the next page results in rich descriptive details. Playing on the enriched surfaces, the light builds them up as the real and palpable limits of the sculptural mass. In this way the heavy bulk of the statue is animated, and a renewal of the ancient sculptural tradition is achieved.

TWO MALE FIGURES BEARING RIVER OFFERINGS. *Dynasty XII.* *p. 77*

As in the *Sphinx of Amenemhet III* (page 75) the unusual type and provenance (from Tanis) of this work led to the original conjecture that it was Hyksos, rather than entirely Egyptian, in origin. Yet this work has also been dated in the time of Amenemhet III. The pair of bearded figures bearing offerings of river fish probably represents the "Niles," or the Nile of Upper Egypt and the Nile of Lower Egypt, portrayed as twin genies. The heavily emphasized construction of the torsos harmonizes with the three-dimensional composition formed by the out-thrust arms bearing the offerings and the symbolically represented rivers. The still-life of the fish and water plants provides the opportunity to vary the surface and allows the light to build up an unusual and complex effect.

PORTRAIT OF AMENEMHET III. *Dynasty XII.*

From Amenemhet III's reign come an unusually extensive series of portrait statues with readily identifiable features: a prominent jaw, sunken eyes, and a broad, strongly marked nose. These works are abundant enough to be classified according to styles associated with specific geographic centers, although there may be some doubt in a few cases.

Compared to the rough and aggressive tone of Tanite figures, this piece from the Fayum, carved in soft limestone, has a different significance. The touch of theatricality which we saw in another work from the Fayum, the *Amenemhet III in Priestly Costume,* is absent here. Instead there is a delicate play of light and shade on the lightly identified features of the face. The delicacy of the conception is also seen in the refined representation of the cord and amulet around the neck, which bring out the unemphatic play of the muscles. This ability to use marginal values and nuances belongs to the classical tradition. The new element, however, is the delicacy in the portrayal of an individual. The richness in human content of Egyptian art. is shown by the coexistence in a single monument of widely divergent attitudes that make a harmonious whole.

Portrait of the Spirit (Ka) of King Hor
Dynasty XII; late nineteenth century B.C.
Wood with traces of gilt; height 5' 9".
From Dashur. (259)

PORTRAIT OF THE SPIRIT (KA) OF KING HOR. *Dynasty XII.*

This statue was found enclosed in a tabernacle in a shaft tomb near the pyramids of Amenèmhet III at Dashur. It represents the spirit or *Ka* of a sovereign named Hor, who does not figure on the dynastic lists but was probably a co-regent of Amenemhet III. He was buried in the vicinity of the more important ruler's tomb. The hieroglyph for the word *Ka* shows two raised arms, hence the crowning element of the statue. As is sometimes the case in wooden statuary, the figure is nude. Originally, a royal loincloth must have been draped around it. Aside from some differences in technique, the statue is a return to the general scheme of wooden sculpture in the Memphite age. In the latter, however, the sculptors often took advantage of the technique to break out of or broaden the formulas; whereas here the ritual theme has perhaps led to the limitations of a clear and facile formalism. That this work is contemporary with more mature and complex sculpture shows that the traditional forms continued to be valued and taught in the art schools.

DANCING DWARFS. *Dynasty XII.*

These three little figures of dwarfs (with a fourth now in the Metropolitan Museum, New York) make up a curious ensemble. They are mounted on round revolving bases that are set into a large base. By pulling a string coiled around them, they can be made to dance. The work has been conceived more or less as a toy. But the possibility of rotary movement, with an infinite succession of points of view, inspires a sculptural quality stemming from within the figures that is not conditioned by a fixed viewpoint. This freedom from any preordained scheme is seen in the disregard for the traditional forms of the body, in the pungently individual faces and in the large beads of the necklaces, which enliven the surface movements of the figures. Although this piece is roughly contemporary with *Head of a Woman With Separate Wig* and the *Cube Statue of Hetep the Treasurer,* all three are unique, revealing the rich variety of themes in Middle Kingdom art.

Dancing Dwarfs
Beginning of Dynasty XII; twentieth
century B.C.
Statuettes in ivory; height 3″.
From a tomb at Lisht.

SARCOPHAGUS OF QUEEN KAWYT. *Dynasty XI.*

In this scene carved on the sarcophagus of a princess in Mentuhotep's court, the queen is seated on a throne with arms, holding a cup to her lips with her right hand and a mirror in her left. Behind her, a maid ties the curls of her wig; in front, a manservant pours her a drink. The words with which he wishes her well appear in hieroglyphics between them. The spacious composition, with figures composed in breadth, and a lively feeling for the contour lines (note the hands of the women dressing the wig) convey a sure mastery of expression. The Memphite formulas have been discarded; there is an intense interest in the profiles and the dynamism they lend to the narrative development.

Sarcophagus of Queen Kawyt
Detail.
Dynasty XI.
White limestone.
From Deir el Bahari (Thebes). (623)

The Daughter of Thuthotep
Dynasty XII; twentieth century B.C.
Painted limestone; height 30″.
From El Bersheh.

THE DAUGHTER OF THUTHOTEP. *Dynasty XII.*

In this painted relief from Thuthotep's tomb, the monarch's daughters are seen in procession. An abstract note is struck by the broad spaces between the figures, the identically repeated gesture of the hand and the flower, the identical shape of the idealized bodies, and the care with which the complicated floral wreaths and the trinkets are rendered. The precision and sureness of composition continues the somewhat tart vigorousness of the reliefs on the *Sarcophagus of Queen Kawyt.*

Sesostris I and the God Horus
Beginning of Dynasty XII; 1971–1928 B.C.
Limestone; width 3′ 6″.
From a destroyed temple at Karnak.

SESOSTRIS I AND THE GOD HORUS.   *Dynasty XII.*

Many temples were constructed during the Middle Kingdom. In almost all cases, successive pharaohs enlarged the existing temples so radically that the old buildings disappeared, or at best were incorporated into the new temples. A pavilion temple of Sesostris I, used as fill in one of the pylons of a Nineteenth Dynasty temple at Karnak, has been extracted and reconstructed in its entirety. A series of architectural members, including the present piece, were also recovered from the foundations. These pillars are from a small temple erected by Sesostris I to commemorate his jubilee, and are of the same type as the reconstructed pavilion. This is small-scale architecture, allowing visitors to circulate in the interior, in contrast to earlier buildings which were meant to be seen primarily from the outside. The pillars repeat in various forms the theme of the king being embraced by different gods, a gesture indicating that he partakes of their divinity. In this example the god is Horus, a hawk god with a human body and the

The Crown of Princess Sat-Hathor-Iunyt
Dynasty XII; period of Sesostris II —
1897–1887 B.C.
Gold and semiprecious stones; height 18 1/2″.
From the tomb of the princess at
Illahun. (52641)

84

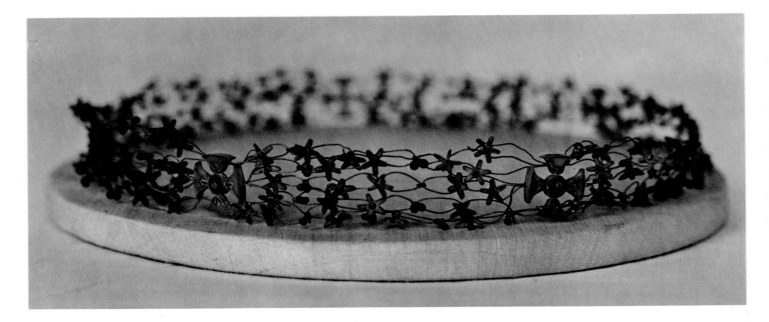

The Crown of Princess Khnumyt
Dynasty XII; nineteenth century B.C.
Gold and semiprecious stones;
circumference 22 1/2".
From the tomb of the princess at
Dashur. (52859)

Pectoral With the Name of Amenemhet III
Dynasty XII; 1847–1797 B.C.
Gold and semiprecious stones; height 3".
From Dashur. (52003)

bird of prey's head. The king wears on his head the insignia of his royalty: the combined crowns of Upper and Lower Egypt. The functional character of this relief is obvious. As a surface decoration it emphasizes the architectural nature of the member on which it is carved, and is meant to be grasped at first glance. The clean-cut edges of the figures are designed to cast a sharp shadow devoid of any nuance, and are in harmony with the lightly incised internal details. The composition is limpidly clear in the disposition of the figures and their contrast to the ground. The smaller design of the hieroglyphs enlivens the schematic austerity of the composition, which was conceived as a figured commentary on the simple volume of a monolithic pillar.

THE CROWN OF PRINCESS SAT-HATHOR-IUNYT. *Dynasty XII.*

p. 85

The princess to whom this crown belonged lived during the reign of Sesostris II, that is, in the early years of the Twelfth Dynasty. The crown consists of a gold band with fifteen applied rosettes decorated with cornelians, amazonites and lapis lazuli. The royal character of the jewel is recalled by the presence in the front of the uraeus. It is thus a version in metal of the crown on the head of Nofret (page 30), in which the rosettes are much simpler and the white of the band may represent silver (rarer than gold at the time) or cloth. At the back are the two emblematic vertical plumes worn by royal ladies, placed so as to fall on the nape of the neck. There are three gold strips cut to imitate the colored ribbons that decorated their coiffures. To allow the ribbons some play, they are hinged rather than soddered to the band. Although conceived as a sumptuous translation into gold of ordinary, everyday elements, this work has an unusual purity and sobriety of line.

THE CROWN OF PRINCESS KHNUMYT. *Dynasty XII.*

This is probably the masterpiece of Egyptian jewelry, a high point in craftsmanship. The gold has been drawn out into wires that form the *cloisonné* of the semiprecious stones in the petals of the flowers. The golden skein and the apparently casual distribution of the flowers suggest a freedom of expression in composition. An organic reliance on tradition is apparent, however, in the underlying clarity and order of the structure. A comparison with the crown of Princess Sat-Hathor-Iunyt (page 85) shows how the interest in exactness has been replaced by a fantasy that stresses the pure joy of light and color. As in the most developed sculpture of the period, reality is viewed in terms of its organic features and light is used to build and define plastic form.

PECTORAL WITH THE NAME OF AMENEMHET III. *Dynasty XII.*

This pectoral comes from a hoard of jewels found at Dashur in the tomb of Princess Sat-Hathor. The materials used in the work include gold, cornelian and lapis lazuli. The details in blue are not made of bits of turquoise

but of glass paste. The openwork plaque represents a kiosk in the upper part of which the vulture of Nekhbet is seen in flight. A dynastic goddess, she holds in her talons the hieroglyphs for "life" and "duration," which extend down to the king's arms. The king is represented twice, in a mirror image, as he brandishes a cudgel over a kneeling bedouin armed with a dagger and stick. Behind the two images of the king are two hieroglyphs for "life" shown with arms that are waving ceremonial fans to give the Pharaoh the "breath of life." In the center space the name of the king appears twice: Ny-maat-Ra ("lord of all the foreign lands"). Other hieroglyphs designating the barbarians and the goddess also serve as links in the composition. Prodigious in technique, but rather labored in composition, this pectoral is not as elegant as others of the time. In the doubling of the principal figure and the functional equivalence of hieroglyph and figure, however, it is very close to some of the architectonic temple reliefs. Like them, it combines signs and images and is meant to be "read" as much as viewed: the art of composition becomes the art of layout.

HIPPOPOTAMUS. *Dynasty XII.*

A considerable number of such blue ceramic figures of the hippopotamus common in the Nile were made during this period. It is not known whether they had any practical use. Some are shown standing peacefully, while others rear aggressively and show their teeth. Drawn on the bodies of these figures in rapid strokes are the flowers and buds of river plants (in this case there is also a butterfly) which represent the aquatic world in which the animal lives. This spirited device was clearly an accepted convention. This work and other similar examples show with what ease and sureness simplified representation produced compositions that are full of a feeling for reality and a serene pride in workmanship.

Hippopotamus
Dynasty XII; twentieth — eighteenth century B.C.
Blue faience; height 4″.

THE NEW KINGDOM

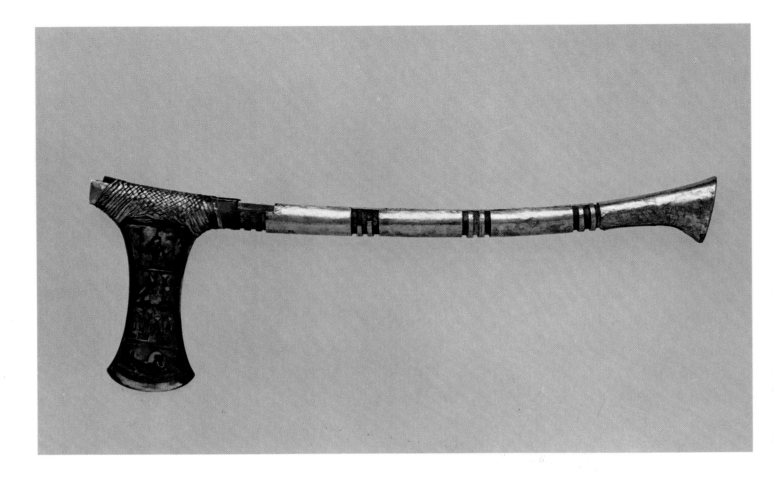

VOTIVE AX. *Dynasty XVIII.*

This ax was found in Queen Ahhotep's sarcophagus, in her tomb at Thebes, along with the military decoration of the "Golden Fly." These two emblems of military honor bestowed on a queen must have been associated with a particular event, and tell us that she had an important and recognized function in public life. The ax bears the name of her son Ahmose, the pharaoh who liberated Egypt from the Hyksos occupation and inaugurated the warlike and imperial New Kingdom — a period during which Egypt's frontiers were extended to the Euphrates on the north and to Nubia on the south, resulting in close contacts with other civilizations which created profound cultural innovations.

The ax was the Egyptian official's parade weapon, whereas the sword and the dagger were the weapons actually used in combat. The ax blade, secured to the handle with a complicated braid of leather thongs, often had surface or openwork decorations. Here there are symbolic representations of the god of eternity, of the two dynastic goddesses shown as heraldic plants of the Nile Valley and the Delta, and finally of a royal sphinx. On the other side of the blade there is a small figure of the king smiting an enemy, and below is the figure of a griffin that is more Minoan than Egyptian in type. The workmanship is not as careful as in Middle Kingdom jewelry, showing that a tradition has been broken and new standards are beginning.

Votive Ax
Beginning of Dynasty XVIII;
circa 1550 B.C.
Copper, gold, semiprecious stones and
glass paste; height of the blade 3″.
From Thebes. (52645)

Head of an Unknown King
Beginning of Dynasty XVIII;
1546–1526 B.C.
Gray volcanic stone; height 8".
From Karnak. (42364)

HEAD OF AN UNKNOWN KING. *Dynasty XVIII.*
Aldred assigned this anonymous head to the Eighteenth Dynasty and
identified it as probably representing Amenophis I, since some of the facial
features resemble those in reliefs of his reign. The pleasingly alert expression is achieved through refinements in the design, such as the carefully
drawn almond shape of the eyes, the sensitive sweep of the eyebrows, and
the upturned corners of the mouth. The warmth of the expression is a new
development, unlike the severe decorum of older royal statues.

91

Head of a Colossal Statue of Thutmose I
Beginning of Dynasty XVIII;
1525–1512 B.C.
Painted limestone; height 3' 11".
From the temple at Karnak.

HEAD OF A COLOSSAL STATUE OF THUTMOSE I. *Dynasty XVIII.*

In the temple at Karnak, which became the national and dynastic shrine of Egypt in the Eighteenth Dynasty, Thutmose I built a passage decorated with pillars. Applied to the pillars were "oyster" statues, that is, figures completely enfolded in a cloak revealing only the head and the hands closed in fists. The heads generally have a long false beard of the type worn by the gods, although the statues are of kings. It is noteworthy that these figures, with their clearly architectonic nature, are set against but not bonded to the pillars. The simplification of the body corresponds to the severity of the architecture with which it harmonizes. Later, when architecture became freer and tended toward movements of light and dark, the colossi lost this simplicity and the figures emerged from their shrouds. Here the faces of the colossal statues are also highly simplified, reduced to clearly defined masses. The strength of the old tradition is seen in this ability to stylize. Eyes, nose and mouth are all larger than life, providing the firm geometric forms that simplify the face, without the small transitions that would disturb the simple treatment of the surface.

SENMUT WITH PRINCESS NEFRURA. *Dynasty XVIII.*

Senmut, tutor of Queen Hatshepsut's daughter, Princess Nefrura, was the Queen's favorite. Senmut was very proud of this honor and had statues

Senmut With Princess Nefrura
Dynasty XVIII; beginning of fifteenth
century B.C.
Black granite; height 4' 3".
From Karnak. (42114)

made of himself with the princess on his knees or in his arms. The cube or block statue that appeared in the Middle Kingdom remained a constant in Egyptian tradition, reappearing from time to time in new forms. The innovations here are in the much more decided schematization of the body, and in the two heads which emerge from the block in different ways. Both are lively and full of curiosity, showing the attractive vitality of the art of the time.

"THE QUEEN OF PUNT." *Dynasty XVIII.*

Stolen from a relief in Queen Hatshepsut's temple at Deir el Bahari (Thebes), this piece was part of an extensive narrative cycle recounting the incidents of the Egyptian expedition by sea to the land of Punt. Legendary for its myrrh trees, ebony, ivory and other tropical goods, Punt was situated somewhere on the Red Sea. The picture cycle marks the beginning of a style tied to specific and exact representation that shows an almost instinctive facility of expression, with a knowing recourse to older solutions. The data of experience has been immediately transcribed in accomplished and formal pictorial language. Emphasis on documentary precision is seen in the portrayal of fish typical of the locality, the dress worn by the natives, and the houses in which they lived. A notable example of this taste for detached observation is the monstrously fat princess, the ethnic character of whose obesity is just as obvious as that of the peculiar costume worn by the male figure next to her.

"The Queen of Punt"
Dynasty XVIII.
Painted limestone.
From the temple of Hatshepsut at Deir el Bahari.

THE PHARAOH THUTMOSE III. *Dynasty XVIII.*
The king advancing and trampling under foot nine arches symbolizing the enemies of Egypt is a theme that dates from the Memphite period. It has been reinterpreted, as can be seen in the broader and more limber stride, the sharp profile, the slimness of the body, and the refined curve of the white crown. This celebrated work illustrates that elegance and confidence were the automatic heritage of centuries of tradition.

THE PHARAOH THUTMOSE III. *Dynasty XVIII.*
Less ambitious than the preceding work, this figure is more composed, in the closed form of the headdress and the heavy false beard that blocks the elegant development of the throat. Traditional and predictable, it also possesses the same ambiguous merits of the other statue. Here perhaps there is a more tranquil relaxation into the hedonism of beautiful physical form (note the tender perfection of the torso), in a frank effort to create a pleasing effect.

95

Queen Isis, The Mother of Thutmose III
Dynasty XVIII; 1482–1450 B.C.
Black granite; height 3′ 3″.
From Karnak. (42072)

Dhewty the Steward
Dynasty XVIII; period of Thutmose III —
1482–1450 B.C.
Black granite; height 33″.
From Karnak. (42123)

QUEEN ISIS, THE MOTHER
OF THUTMOSE III. *Dynasty XVIII.*

Not a queen by full right, Isis was the concubine of Thutmose I. Her statue thus could have been made only when her son finally succeeded to the throne, after a long period as a priest. She appears in all the solemnity of the royal costume, with the uraeus on her forehead and a diadem that probably supported a double plume. In her hand she holds an unidentifiable object. The composition is traditional in pose, dress, and coiffure. It should be noted, however, that the wig is brought forward so as to frame the face in a more marked way than is usual, which emphasizes the linearity of its features.

DHEWTY THE STEWARD. *Dynasty XVIII.*

The theme of a kneeling figure holding a base, supported on his knees, with his hands is an old one. In the early examples, however, the hands (sometimes holding objects) were placed on the knees, to form a clearly defined block. Here the base or pedestal must have held the image of a god or a group of gods, for this is the first instance of a theme that was later to become popular. The addition of elements testifying to Dhewty's piety have adversely affected the quality of the statue, which has lost the possibility of a unified point of view. The minutely described vertical locks of hair and the horizontal waves of the triangular wig falling to the shoulders introduce a note of refined frivolity.

COW FROM DEIR EL BAHARI. *Dynasty XVIII.*   *pp. 98–99*

Although this monument bears the cartouche of Amenophis II, it is from a chapel dedicated to Hathor which was built at Deir el Bahari by his father Thutmose III. The statue thus dates from around the time of the death of Thutmose III. The figure is the patron goddess of the necropolis, who is identified with Hathor and is often represented as a heifer coming from the western mountain — the place where one follows the sun and entombs the dead. Among the papyrus of the ponds at the edge of the desert, Egyptian herds graze freely. The emergence from the mountain (from the "Beautiful West" which was also a divinity) is rendered by representing the papyrus on the head and forequarters of the heifer, to indicate that she is coming through clumps of the plant. The king places himself under her protection, and leans against the divine creature — a composition seen in other works of the period. The sovereign is shown again as an infant suckling directly from the heifer. By drinking her milk, he will be reborn in the next world, over which she presides. The complex symbolism must be borne in mind to understand the meaning of the work. Even more, it makes us appreciate how little the symbolic burden has deflected the artist from viewing this supernatural world through his daily experience, his love of nature, and his faith in life.

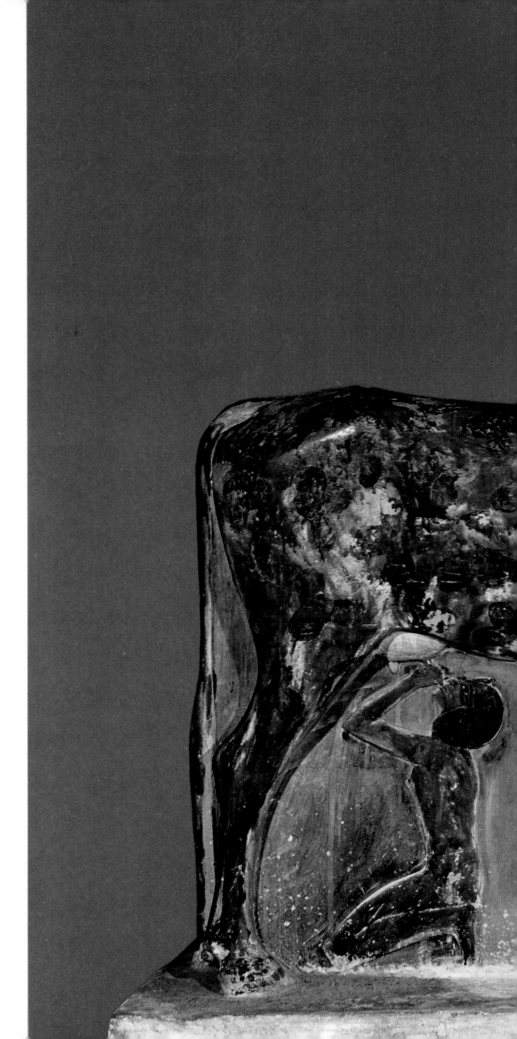

Cow From Deir el Bahari
Dynasty XVIII; circa 1450 B.C.
Painted limestone; length 7′ 5″.
From Deir el Bahari. (38574)

98

THUTMOSE IV AND HIS MOTHER. *Dynasty XVIII.*

There are precedents for representing a king with his mother rather than with his wife; it may have had political significance as well. The group is composed with great sobriety, emphasized by the considerable space between the two figures and the firm embrace of the two arms at the back. The separation of the figures allows them to be treated as single entities, with a rare usefulness and solidity. The bodies are large, firm and powerfully muscled. The coiffures are imposing and heavy; the king's spherical wig is an innovation. In the faces there is none of the fashionable sweetly smiling grace; they are closed, hard-jawed and have narrow little eyes. The weight of gravity in the work suggests fatigue with the sensuality and perfection that was common at the time. This is probably the creation of an austere artist who sought to return to the old ideals.

AMENOPHIS II KNEELING TO MAKE AN OFFERING. *Dynasty XVIII.*

The importance of this royal statue, which shows the king kneeling before the god and presenting on offering table, stems from the fact that it is a new departure in iconography. The heavy relationship of the table and the knees defeats any compositional reality. In the *Two Male Figures Bearing River Offerings* (page 77) from the Middle Kingdom, the out-thrust arms determined a whole system of balances involving an opulently decorative still life; here the artist is only concerned with the cleancut workmanship of the beautiful material and the refined idealization of the king's face.

Above:
Amenophis II Kneeling to Make an Offering
Dynasty XVIII; 1450–1425 B.C.
Gray granite; height 3' 11".
From Karnak. (42073)

Above, left:
Thutmose IV and His Mother
Dynasty XVIII; 1425–1417 B.C.
Black granite; height 3' 7".
From Karnak. (42080)

Second Coffin of Queen Merit Amon
Detail.
Dynasty XVIII; 1450–1425 B.C.
Colored and gilded cedar wood;
height 10' 4".
From Deir el Bahari. (53140)

Amenophis the Wise, Son of Hapu
Dynasty XVIII; reign of Amenophis III —
1417–1379 B.C.
Gray granite; height 4′ 8″.
From Karnak. (42127)

SECOND COFFIN OF QUEEN MERIT AMON. *p. 101*

This gigantic coffin contained the body of the wife of Amenophis II, the daughter of Thutmose III. The tomb was robbed and restored in antiquity; thus the eyes are not original and the missings inlays of semiprecious stones and glass paste have been painted in. It is not, however, the spectacular size, nor the value of the materials, nor the perfection of the cabinet-maker's technique that make this coffin so unusual, but the vitality of the face, in which the surfaces are modulated so as to create a continuous passage from plane to plane. An examination of the mummy proved that this is not a portrait of the Queen. Rather, a search for a tranquil physical beauty coincided here with traditional craftsmanship. It is reminiscent of the organic qualities of a woman's skin in the Middle Kingdom *Head of a Woman with Separate Wig* (page 70). It is in this summation of high skills, whereby extraordinary results are obtained without apparent effort, that one finds the truest accents of the mature Eighteenth Dynasty.

AMENOPHIS THE WISE, SON OF HAPU. *Dynasty XVIII.*

Charm and facility, the pursuit of the pleasing and the beautiful — often the object of Eighteenth Dynasty artists — reached their height in the reign of Amenophis III. The period was also marked by highly diversified developments in form, but in general they shared a hedonistic outlook. Some excellent examples that show an intellectual awareness of their power to please are seen in several statues of Amenophis, son of Hapu. This court dignitary was so dear to the king that he was allowed the unusual honor of a mortuary temple like that of a sovereign. He passed into legend and mythology as a benevolent sage and a helpful god, and was known to the Greeks who later established themselves in Egypt.

This portrait of Amenophis is unusual in that technique is aimed at results very different from those sought by other New Kingdom artists. There are no other instances during the period of the figure's pose — legs crossed to form a geometric block on which the hands rest — but it was known in Middle Kingdom art. The wig and costume are also seen in the Middle Kingdom, whereas there is only a single example from the New Kingdom. Although these details are eloquent, it is even more significant that the face has been given the severe and troubled expression of the royal portrait statues of the earlier period. It is clear that the intention was to repeat the external forms and style of a previous age. In the almost perfect reconstruction there is, however, a refined and sentimental touch.

HEAD OF A KING. *Dynasty XVIII.* *p. 104*

Carved in obsidian, this face of a pharaoh is part of a composite statue, in which the different parts were executed separately and in different mate-

rials. The rough core for attaching the headdress is visible, and the eyes must have been inlaid. The practice of assembling the parts recalls Diodorus' statement that among Egyptian sculptors each executed a part of a statue. The Greek historian, however, was probably referring to sculptural models of later times, which were in fact separate parts of the body. The date of this piece is disputed, and it has been ascribed to reigns ranging from that of Thutmose III to Seti I. The material, a volcanic glass that is one of the most obstinate substances to work, has been mastered with casual ease; note the design of the mouth, which is as fluid as if the material were malleable. This serene virtuosity, even more than a certain resemblance to the Thutmosids, suggests a date in the late Eighteenth Dynasty.

Head of a King
Middle of Dynasty XVIII; fifteenth — fourteenth century B.C.
Obsidian; height 7".
From Karnak. (42101)

TELL EL AMARNA

COLOSSAL STATUES OF IKHNATON. *Dynasty XVIII.*

At the end of the Eighteenth Dynasty a radical revolution took place at the court. In honor of his god, the sovereign, who had acceded to the throne as Amenophis IV, assumed the name of Ikhnaton. He declared that the only god was Aton, the sun, and that his representative on earth was the king, who was thus a demiurge in charge of order in the world. This was a renewal of the old theological tradition respecting royal divinity. To it was added the moral heritage of the importance of charity in the world, which had become a part of Egyptian thinking in the New Kingdom. The king's conscious and aggressive solar monotheism was the point of departure for a series of reforms aimed at reinforcing what was as against what should be. In language, the colloquial replaced the scholastic tradition. Clothes that were really worn ordinarily took the place of special parade dress. And in representations of the king, he was shown in everyday situations rather than posed in terms of rigid official symbolism. The aim of this innovation was to dramatize the beginning of a new era, and in fact the violent break with the past has no other historical parallel.

This outspoken challenge is seen in the group of some thirty colossal statues from the temple at Karnak, where the king had erected elaborate buildings for the worship of his god in the very sanctuary of the fearful god Amon, whom he sought to eliminate. These are works of the earliest years of his reign, probably during the co-regency with his father, and the new elements are particularly elaborate. The statues stand against pillars; the architectonic feeling is maintained by showing them in sheathe-like clothes and by treating the faces as a system of broad planes. In these two statues, on the contrary, the king is shown in royal dress that leaves much of his body bare, with a strong play of light and shade featured. Each statue has a different headdress, and ornaments like necklaces and bracelets which in other works were little more than incised on the body and the dress, are vigorously molded and stand out here. Even more provocative is the way in which the king's physique has been treated. The face has been given an abstract expression, and the thinness of the torso emphasizes the pot belly and the big hips. A physical type has been constructed which is the exact opposite of the classical Egyptian model — with its broad chest and shoulders, flat belly and lithe hips. The tangle of elements, the breaking of surfaces, sharp cutting and energetic contours no longer confined to a single modulated line — all send the light charging back and forth in movements suggesting emotion and vitality.

The discovery that it is valid to use all artistic means of expression is a reflection of the revolution in art. It is the value placed on daily life that makes the works of this period so modern in feeling, and plants the seed for later Egyptian art. These Theban colossi, perhaps sculpted by Bak, are eloquent and meaningful as a manifesto of the early revolution.

Colossal Statues of Ikhnaton
Dynasty XVIII; 1379–1362 B.C.
Sandstone with traces of polychromy;
height of each statue 13′ 1″.
From Karnak. (49528, 49529)

KING IKHNATON AND HIS FAMILY
ADORING THE GOD ATON. *Dynasty XVIII*.

This relief from the royal tomb shows the king, his wife Nefertiti, and their two daughters worshiping Aton. The elder princess sounds the sistrum with one hand and holds her sister by the other. The king and queen offer flowers to the sun, which is represented above as a disk, with the traditional uraeus. The sun's rays turn into arms to indicate that all work is connected with the god, and terminate in hands, some of which hold the symbol of "life." Below are stands holding flowers as offerings.

From internal evidence the work has been dated early in Ikhnaton's reign, perhaps the ninth year. The general compositional scheme is immediately apparent: it is based on a triangle, formed by the figures, which rises from the little princesses to the god. The carving of the relief varies in depth and expressiveness depending on the importance of what is being represented. Thus the focal point of the composition lies in the upper right-hand corner. The irregular distribution of the light on the surfaces is accompanied by the movements created by the lines of hieroglyphics, the flowers, the altars, and the rays of the god. These are all elements that create ground figures of minor intensity and interest with respect to the main subjects of the composition. A comparison with reliefs in which the hiero-

King Ikhnaton and His Family
Adoring the God Aton
Dynasty XVIII; ninth year of Ikhnaton's reign — 1370 B.C.
Limestone island relief with traces of color; height and width 19″ x 20″.
From Tell el Amarna. (54517)

glyphics and figures are equivalents, as in the *Portrait of the Court Official Hesira* (page 55), and *Sesostris I and the God Horus* (page 69), stresses the rich play of light that this solution offers. The effect of vitality created by light in the colossi of Karnak is also evident here. In keeping with the lively light effects is the fluent and nervous contour of the bodies, which follows a most unusual canon. The supports do not appear equal to the weights they bear: heads are big, necks small, while the prominent bellies and big hips are carried on thin legs and slender ankles. The profiles are unnaturally shaped and characterized so as to make a continually moving contour line.

IKHNATON WITH AN OFFERING TABLET. *Dynasty XVIII.*

A band from the front of the crown, and the uraeaus, are missing from this statue. They may have been made of gold, which would explain the theft. The king, probably Ikhnaton, carries a tablet on which flowers and food of different kinds are laid out in orderly fashion. An unusual note are the sandals, which show the king's insistence on being portrayed in ordinary, everyday dress. Another significant fact is that the feet are shown together, which was the rule in statues of women but not of men. Also, the figure is painted in yellow ocher, the color for women, rather than in

Ikhnaton With an Offering Tablet
Dynasty XVIII; 1379–1362 B.C.
Colored limestone on an alabaster base;
height 15 3/4".
From Tell el Amarna. (43580)

109

the brick red used for men. Bringing the feet together has reduced the supporting base of the composition but makes a counterpoint to the over-balance of the extended arms and slab. To contemporary Egyptians, the work must have appeared singularly unstable. A similar gesture in *Two Male Figures Bearing River Offerings* (page 77) led to a totally different compositional solution. It is in its dynamic structure that the great interest of this little statue lies.

QUEEN NEFERTITI (?).   *Dynasty XVIII.*
The head of this work must have belonged to a statue composed of various parts: the neck has a nub to fit into a socket, and the crown of the head must have been covered by a wig in another material. The head itself was obviously never completed. There are clearly visible guidelines drawn by the artist halfway down the brow, along the nose, and on the eyes. As Egyptian sculptors worked on a figure, they repainted on the block — in ever more minute detail — the effect that they wanted to obtain. Models were not used, but these successive refinements kept the artist in close contact with the work. An indication of this familiarity here is that the mouth has been painted, while the rest of the face remains to be finished.

In a work such as this many of the provocative features of the earlier statues have disappeared. There is no longer the sour pleasure in empha-sizing unpleasant traits, nor the defiant and scandalous tone. It is also apparent that there is nothing left of the hedonistic pleasure in representa-tion of the Eighteenth Dynasty. The physical beauty of the face is entirely incidental and is not the subject of the work. The interest here is in seizing the fluctuating aspects of the surfaces and interpreting their structure with-out rigidly defining them. Note the treatment of the eye, which is defin-itely marked off only above. The light that reveals the vitality of this face is the means by which the artist expressed his imagination. We have here the last echo of what was heralded in the *Colossal Statues of Ikhnaton* (pages 106–107) at Karnak, but the abstract and rigid formulations have been transmuted into the reality of life and things. If we may associate the name of the sculptor Bak with the first period of the revolution, that of Thutmose may be identified with this more mature and complex phase. Thutmose's studio was discovered at Tell el Amarna, where the king had his residence. The numerous works found in the studio exemplify the new art, with its serene balance between vigorous inspiration and the progres-sive dissolution of any schematic program in the execution of the work.

HEAD OF A PRINCESS.   *Dynasty XVIII.*   *p. 112*
This small head is related to a number of others in various museums that portray the daughters of Ikhnaton. This one is a fragment of a composite statue, as are some of the others. The ability to utilize light for a loving exploration of reality, which we have seen in the head of the Queen (page 111), is shown here more blandly and immediately. There is also a more explicit statement of such features as the sinuous profile, the shape of the

110

Queen Nefertiti (?)
Dynasty XVIII; fourteenth century B.C. Unfinished work; in quartzite with indica-tions in color; height 13″.
From Tell el Amarna. (59286)

mouth, and the anomalous development of the head. This last translates the traditional top-heavy heads of the monarchs wearing tall crowns into an anatomical peculiarity. These are all elements that recall the first period of the "revolution." They are combined in the face with a harmony that does not degenerate into sweetness. It is this coherency of object that separates this head from the facile gracefulness of the Eighteenth Dynasty.

Head of a Princess
Fragment.
Dynasty XVIII; fourteenth century B.C.
Rose quartzite; height 13".
From Tell el Amarna. (44869)

KING IKHNATON KISSING HIS CO-REGENT. *Dynasty XVIII.*
This is the first representation in the round of a sovereign in the lap of the goddess whose son he claims to be. In religious terms, it probably indicates that Ikhnaton had taken Smenhkkara, his co-regent during his last years, into the world of his divinity. This interpretation seems more likely than another which is often given: that the group shows the king kissing one of his daughters. Family affection among royalty, however, was a common theme during this period, in marked contrast to the pharaohs' complete detachment from sentiment in earlier ages. This unfinished

King Ikhnaton Kissing His Co-Regent
Dynasty XVIII; 1379–1362 B.C.
Limestone, unfinished; height 17″.
From Tell el Amarna. (44866)

work comes from the studio of the sculptor Thutmose. It shows the merits of a solid, volumetric composition that respects the geometric basis of Egyptian art even at its most untraditional.

CANOPIC JAR (OF MERIT-ATON?). *Dynasty XVIII.*

Canopic jars are the funeral urns in which the entrails of the body were stored after they were extracted during the process of mummification. The remains were placed under the protection of four divinities — who were represented sculpturally in classical times on the lids of four vessels — in the guise of a man, a dog, a baboon and a hawk. During the age of reform, profound changes occurred in the funeral ritual, and the lids of the four canopic jars were given human heads representing the deceased. It has been suggested that this example is from the tomb of Smenhkkara. The jar, however, shows traces of having been reworked. The coiffure is rather feminine, which suggests that it be attributed to one of the princesses of Tell el Amarna.

The piece shows great refinement in the contrast of worked and smooth surfaces, and in the soberly elegant rendering of the face. If there is a suggestion of journeyman work, it is in the slight recollection of the elegant effects of the period immediately preceding the reform.

DUCKS IN A SWAMP. *Dynasty XVIII.*

Many of the floors of the royal palace at Tell el Amarna are decorated with paintings. In the main hall especially, there are numerous remains of open-air scenes with detailed descriptions of plants, birds and animals. It is painting of a free and unschematic sort, with a fresh use of color, rapidly brushed in, without contour lines. This floor painting had a practical as well as a decorative purpose: it was to be walked on and was intended to enliven a civic building. But the relaxed feeling for color as a valid means of evoking barely indicated forms is the summation of many attempts in the past — bold effects that were used only marginally and on a small scale. Here, too, light as color succeeds in giving a feeling of life, even in the rather obvious compositional rhythms of the fanned-out plants.

THE SECOND COFFIN
OF TUTANKHAMON. *Dynasty XVIII.* *p. 116*

Three coffins were used to store the body of Tutankhamon. The first was of gilded wood; the second, gilded wood with glass paste; the third, massive gold. The king is shown in this second coffin with the royal headdress

Canopic Jar (*of Merit-Aton?*)
Dynasty XVIII; fourteenth century B.C.
Alabaster, with inlaid eyes; height 7".
From the Valley of the Kings (Thebes).
(3610)

Ducks in a Swamp
Dynasty XVIII; fourteenth century B.C.
Tempera painting.
From Tell el Amarna (Hawata).

and the attributes of the god Osiris, to whom he is assimilated on dying. The glass-paste decoration takes the form of wings, which have a religious significance. The coffin belongs to perhaps the most famous archaeological discovery ever made. In the infinite variety of the objects found by the excavators, there is a lavish display of the arts and crafts of the Eighteenth Dynasty. It is the most refined moment in Egyptian art, and follows the shock of the Amarna revolution.

THE GOLDEN COFFIN OF TUTANKHAMON. *Dynasty XVIII.*

This is perhaps the most celebrated object in the history of goldsmith's work. It is made of approximately 450 pounds of gold. The superb craftsmanship of this glittering work has been applied to a design inspired mainly by late Eighteenth-Dynasty art, but some elements certainly stem from Tell el Amarna.

Below, right:
The Second Coffin of Tutankhamon
Detail.
Post-Amarna period;
Dynasty XVIII, 1361–1352 B.C.
Gilded wood with inlays of glass paste;
length 6′ 7″.
From Tutankhamon's tomb in the
Valley of the Kings.

Below, left:
The Golden Coffin of Tutankhamon
Post-Amarna period; Dynasty XVIII,
1361–1352 B.C.
Gold with inlays of semiprecious stones
(cornelians, lapis lazuli, turquoises);
length 5′ 11″.
From Tutankhamon's tomb in the
Valley of the Kings. (Carter 255)

Right: detail.

STATUE OF TUTANKHAMON. *Dynasty XVIII.*
A curious piece, this statue has no legs and the arms are cut off at the armpits. There are no details of musculature or dress. It has been suggested that this is an example of the private statuary that was made to serve as cult images of the dead, which had only a head and trunk without any details. The face is of a type known at Tell el Amarna, with a swelling mouth and a sinuous development of the features. There is also a generalized and pleasing rotundity that reflects tradition as well as current practice.

Statue of Tutankhamon
Post-Amarna period; Dynasty XVIII,
1361–1352 B.C.
Stuccoed and painted wood, inlaid eyes;
height 17".
From Tutankhamon's tomb in the
Valley of the Kings.

118

Tutankhamon Hurling a Harpoon
Post-Amarna period; Dynasty XVIII.
1361–1352 *B.C.*
Gilded wood, painted green boat;
height 28″.
From Tutankhamon's tomb in the
Valley of the Kings. (T. 407)

TUTANKHAMON HURLING A HARPOON. *Dynasty XVIII.*
Other examples of this subject are seen in the remains of older royal boats, which also showed the sovereign on a hippopoatmus hunt, standing in a light craft made of bundles of reeds, and about to launch a harpoon. The probable religious significance is that the scene recalls the myth of Horus, the harpooner, and Seth, who was transformed into a hippopotamus. The new elements here are the concavity of the kilt, which gives the figure an unusual movement, the sandals and the pot belly. These significant details are typical of Tell el Amarna.

Shrine of Tutankhamon's Canopic Jars
Post-Amarna period; Dynasty XVIII,
1362–1352 B.C.
Gilded wood; 6′ 7″ x 4 ′1″ x 5′ 0″.
From Tutankhamon's tomb in the
Valley of the Kings.

Right: detail showing the goddess Selkit.

SHRINE OF TUTANKHAMON'S CANOPIC JARS. *Dynasty XVIII.*
pp. 120–121

This elaborate construction of a shrine under a canopy was made to contain the canopic jars for the king's entrails. The repeated uraeus motif echoing the curves of the two moldings at the top follows a tradition that dates from the Third Dynasty. Here, however, it provides a crowning element that appears to flicker, and thus lightens the structure.

The most appealing and elegant part of the shrine is the disposition of the four small statues of goddesses who protect the canopic jars (only two are visible here). The goddesses, who make protective gestures, are placed at the sides rather than carved at the corners, as in simpler models. This technique of lightening architectonic effects by the use of statues is thorougly exploited in later Ramessid architecture.

Although the statuette of the goddess Selkit (page 121) is an integral part of the shrine, it is worth examining it separately in order to see how the revolutionary elements of Tell el Amarna have been utilized to lend elegance and grace. The proportions of the body, the intense expression of the face, the slim attenuated arms, and the gaze that increases the sense of space by wandering outside the expected direction — all are fluently pleasing aspects of this figure that relate to the tradition of the age of Amenophis III.

Painted Chest with Scene of Tutankhamon Battling Asians
Post-Amarna period; Dynasty XVIII.
Painted wood; height 19″.
From Tutankhamon's tomb in the Valley of the Kings. (Carter 21)

Right: detail.

PAINTED CHEST WITH SCENE OF
TUTANKHAMON BATTLING ASIANS. *Dynasty XVIII.*

Tutankhamon — "more valorous there is none second to him" says the text — is shown here in an imaginary battle with Asians. Much larger than the other figures, he occupies the center of the composition. The play of the saddlecloth, feathers and ribbons gives more movement to what is otherwise an entirely conventional scheme. More interesting is the advance behind the king of the Egyptian cavalry in a landscape with plants that recalls *Ducks in a Swamp* (page 115). Even more impressive, however, is the complicated and dynamic aerial perspective of the fallen enemy. As in earlier works, the enemy is seen as undignified; the new element is the warm and vital tangle of bodies.

SHRINE OF THE STATUES
OF THE ROYAL COUPLE. *Dynasty XVIII.*

This wooden tabernacle sheathed in gold probably contained the massive gold statues of the royal couple, which were stolen long ago. The bars for bolting the shrine are made of ebony. The whole work is mounted on a simulated silver-sheathed ledge, to indicate the funerary character of an object that has to be "dragged" into the tomb. On the walls of the shrine, the decoration shows variations on the theme of conjugal affection: the queen is shown dressing or anointing the seated king. In other panels the king is the active figure, while the queen crouches on a stool at his feet. The harem idea continues a theme from Tell el Amarna, whereby the king was shown enjoying ordinary family pleasures. This theme also appears in later Ramessid art. In this example it achieves the maximum in conscious, sensual sentimentality. The highly detailed descriptions of dress — ribbons, folds, crowns, jewels — are a first experiment in applying to body coverings the effects of light that had been worked out at Tell el Amarna on the living surfaces of the bodies themselves.

The two panels from the shrine reproduced on page 125 are very different in subject. The upper panel has an intimate, refined grace. The lower adopts the official tone of the offering of the "sign of the year," from which hangs the sign for "100,000." The gods are often shown offering this "sign of the year" to the king. The difference in theme changes the attitudes of the figures, but the mode of treating the surface so that there is a continual variation in light remains the same.

Shrine of the Statues of the Royal Couple
Post-Amarna period; Dynasty XVIII.
Gold-sheathed wood, sledge runners
sheathed in silver;
height of each panel 5 1/2″.
From the tomb of Tutankhamon in the
Valley of the Kings.

Right: detail.

LID OF A COFFER WITH HAREM SCENE. *Dynasty XVIII.*

The subject developed in the Amarna period of the queen offering flowers to the king, who leans languidly on a staff, has been vulgarized and impoverished here. Much of the meaning of the composition has been obliterated by the luxuriant floral background. In the band below, the scene showing the gathering of mandrake adds charming secondary motifs to the already complicated and elegant decoration.

126

Lid of a Coffer With Harem Scene
Post-Amarna period; Dynasty XVIII.
Wood with ivory inlay; 12 1/2″ x 7 3/4″.
From Tutankhamon's tomb in the
Valley of the Kings. (Carter 540)

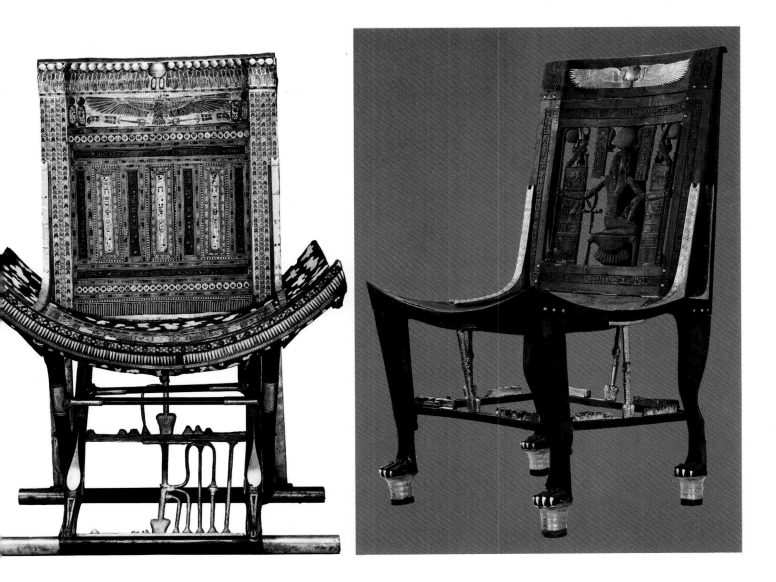

CHAIRS. *Dynasty XVIII.*

Both chairs are refined examples of the cabinetmaker's art, and could have been made only for a royal household. The one on the left is an elaborate version of the folding chair, with the goose-head feet customary in this type. The seat and the back are not well suited to a folding chair, but their use was obligatory because of religious associations. The detailed, trite decoration has obviously been used for the display of a craftsman's virtuosity.

The other example (right) has the classic form of Egyptian chairs, which was adopted during the Napoleonic era and spread all over Europe. The design is perfectly functional, and the old magic motif of the lion's feet has been felicitously included in this practical piece of furniture. On the back, the god of eternity is shown protecting the name of Tutankhamon with the sign of the "year." One can see vestiges of the heraldic decoration that ornamented the throne of Chephren (page 33).

Chairs
Post-Amarna period; Dynasty XVIII.

127

THRONE WITH
TUTANKHAMON AND QUEEN. *Dynasty XVIII.*

The new artistic currents from Tell el Amarna are apparent in the intimate and unrhetorical scene on this throne, in the loose-limbed figures with their slight but studied awkwardness, and in the dynamic relationship between the king and queen. It may seem somewhat incongruous that so much art and energy should have gone into the decoration of a chair back. Yet a closer look shows how the theme and the details betray a certain sweetness that is the opposite of the direction of Amarna art. The great popularity that this piece has always enjoyed is an indication of its basically artisan character.

Throne With Tutankhamon and Queen
Post-Amarna period; Dynasty XVIII.
Wood plated with gold and silver, inlays of glass paste; 21″ x 21″.
From Tutankhamon's tomb in the Valley of the Kings. (Carter 91)

Right: detail of the back.

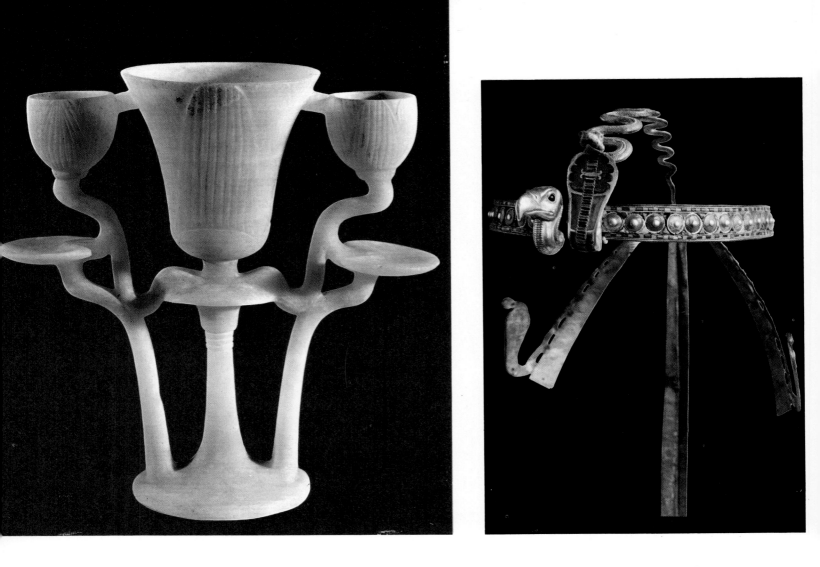

FLORAL VASE. *Dynasty XVIII.*

The designs that appear on the inside in transparency on numerous alabaster floral vases indicate that they may have been intended as lamps. Here the aquatic plant motif, with its soft sinuous curves, is a graceful note taken from reality and developed with suave refinement. In this way, the innovations in form at the end of the Eighteenth Dynasty were utilized by artisans.

A ROYAL CROWN. *Dynasty XVIII.*

This crown follows the model of Princess Sat-Hathor-Iunyt's crown (page 85) but has no plumes, which are more a feminine adjunct. The uraeus is accompanied by a vulture's head, recalling the two dynastic goddesses of Upper and Lower Egypt — one takes the form of a vulture, and the other of a cobra.

DAGGER AND SHEATH. *Dynasty XVIII.*

The blade of this dagger is made of iron and is one of the earliest examples of the use of this material in ancient Egypt. A palmetto motif in the Syrian mode decorates the side of the sheath shown here. The same Syrian influence, even more marked, is seen on the other side, where animals are represented in a flying gallop.

130

Above, left:
Floral Vase
Post-Amarna period; Dynasty XVIII.
Alabaster; height 11".
From Tutankhamon's tomb in the
Valley of the Kings.

Above, right:
A Royal Crown
Post-Amarna period; Dynasty XVIII.
Gold, cornelian, lapis lazuli, turquoise;
height 15".
From Tutankhamon's tomb in the
Valley of the Kings.

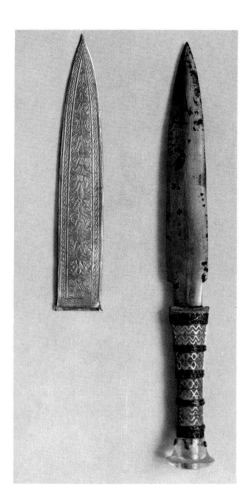

THE GOD KHONSU. *Dynasty XVIII–XIX.*

This statue of the youngest god of the Theban triad illustrates the influence of the revolutionary Amarna period on the Tutankhamon-Harmais age and the beginning of the following dynasty. The god is shown standing, swathed in the Osirian garb through which are seen the anatomical details of the knees and the complete outline of the arms. The hands hold the royal symbols of a whip and a pastoral staff, and a complicated vertical scepter bearing the signs of "stability," "life" and "duration." In addition to the collar incised around the neck in the old style, there is a large necklace executed in relief. The false beard is an attribute of the gods, and the large sidelock is part of the traditional coiffure of children and princes of the blood. So many details of dress and symbolism, all plastically treated, recall the artist's approach in the *Colossal Statues of Ikhnaton* (pages 106–107). But here the sculptor does not presume to alter the beauty of the body. The face reflects Tutankhamon's physical type, and there is a touch of sentiment in the half-shut eyes and the sinuous, bee-stung mouth. A more obvious influence from Amarna is seen in the shadows on the cheeks and at the corners of the mouth.

PORTRAIT OF THAI AND NAIA. *Dynasty XIX.*

In type, this group statue of a married couple could belong to the end of the Eighteenth Dynasty. That period could have produced the husband's wig in two tiers, falling to his breast, as well as the wife's, with its mass of braids. The same is true of the simplicity of the costumes, especially the woman's. However, a certain difficulty of expression and rusticity signify that the mechanical felicity of the Eighteenth Dynasty has been left behind. Some of the old modes reappear: the folds on the belly of the man, to state anatomical demarcations; the indifference to the features of the faces, which are practically the same in both figures; and the geometric form of the volumes. A new and more modest beginning has been made. The old traditions have been investigated again, without the brashness of the artist who seeks to show himself superior to his teacher. The interest is in rediscovering the tradition against which Tell el Amarna had rebelled.

Portrait of Thai and Naia
Pre-Ramessid period; beginning of Dynasty XIX, fourteenth century B.C.
Limestone; height 35″.
From the necropolis at Sakkara. (628)

THE RAMESSID AGE

STATUE OF RAMESSES II. *Dynasty XIX.*

Many portraits of Ramesses II have survived, ranging from those of moderate size to the colossi of Abu Simbel and the Ramesseum. In the course of the Pharaoh's very long life he assiduously employed the artistic talent of the country. This bust closely resembles another statue of the king in Turin. Both have the surface vibrations, created by the myriad of pleats fanning out, that function outside the structural system of the figure. In the head, where two spherical masses are conjoined, the smooth surface of the face contrasts with the minutely represented locks of hair. The lesson of Amarna — that light is the vital element — was the point of departure for this new view. A comparison with the earlier statue of Thutmose IV (page 100) shows what a radical change took place in Egyptian art in little more than a century, thanks to the impulse deriving from the Ikhnaton period.

STATUETTE OF HORI THE PRIEST. *Dynasty XIX.*   *p. 136*

In this wooden statuette, the whole composition turns on the contrast between the head, which is bald and carefully individualized, and the costume or vestments. It is more than an intellectual exercise in opposites because of the characterization of the head and the three-dimensional rhythms of the vestments that completely conceal the body. Spatial effects are seen in the elegant elaboration of complex but perfectly organic contours, like that which runs from the narrowing of the sleeve to the widening of the apron below. Here the play of light and shade is aimed at creating a complex rather than a self-contained structure. In the Middle Kingdom, light was used to reveal the organic quality of a mass. Now the counterpoint of equally valid masses emphasizes the dynamism that comes from the new feeling for space. Space is seen as the ground for living action and not as an intellectual means for the placing of a plastic mass.

BUST OF A PRINCESS
OF THE TIME OF RAMESSES II. *Dynasty XIX.*   *p. 137*

On her head, the princess wears a heavy wig, made up of minute locks of hair, that is secured by a metal band with two sacred asps or cobras at the front. One of the symbolic snakes wears the crown of Upper Egypt, the other the crown of Lower Egypt. On top of the wig is set a diadem on which the uraeus, with the solar disk, is repeated. Originally this circlet must have supported two plumes or the cow horns of the goddess Hathor. There are two large gold earrings in the ears, and around the neck is a necklace made up of signs for "beautiful." Another necklace, with a counterweight in the form of the head of a divinity, is held in the hand, following court usage whereby members of the royal entourage saluted the Pharoah by waving such necklaces. Two rosettes cover the nipples. All these details enabled the artist to build up the contrast between the com-

Statue of Ramesses II
Fragment.
Dynasty XIX; 1304–1237 B.C.
Gray granite; height 30".
From Tanis. (616)

135

plicated decorations and the limpid simplicity of the face, which appears to loom out of its luxurious trappings.

In general form, the work is similar to the preceding figure, but in addition has polychromy and plays more on associative ideas and feelings. It justifies the broad definition of this period as the "Egyptian Baroque."

Statuette of Hori the Priest
Dynasty XIX; thirteenth century B.C.
Wood with traces of color; height 8″.
From Sakkara. (805)

Bust of a Princess
of the Time of Ramesses II
Dynasty XIX; 1304–1237 B.C.
Polychromed limestone; height 30″.
From Thebes, the Ramesseum. (600)

FUNERAL PROCESSION. *Dynasty XIX.*

The vitality of the Ramessid age shows its most interesting and appealing results in relief and painting rather than in sculpture in the round, in which the weight of tradition and technique was greater. In painting especially, the drive to tell a story and represent a situation, rather than to portray one or more figures, had been since the beginning of Egyptian civilization a constant element of tension contrasting with the formal, official tradition. This latent vitality found in the free manner of sculpting and painting that was taught at Tell el Amarna the formal representational means to express its informal impulses. The light and the profiles that are used to render a dynamic view are the point of departure for a much less trite and precise way of drawing. Often there is no concern with connecting the various elements of the narrative. But the whole work, precisely because of

Funeral Procession
Dynasty XIX.
Painted sandstone; height 29 1/2″.
From Thebes.

its "colloquial" character, expresses the moving, dramatic and dynamic quality of a situation. In this scene of people walking in a funeral procession, the figures move forward in different ways, are constructed according to different canons of proportion, and are in general shown as diverse within their similar actions. Going beyond the balances of the composition, the work succeeds in giving an impression of movement and reality that had been virtually unknown in Egyptian art.

DANCE SCENE. *Dynasty XIX*.

This work is probably part of a cycle of funerary scenes from a destroyed tomb. The ancient Egyptians' gift for composition is evident in the overall division of the men and the women dancers into two halves and then in the subdivisions made by the trios of women. The centralized group in the

Dance Scene
Dynasty XIX; thirteenth century B.C.
Painted limestone; height 16″.
From Sakkara. (562)

139

center, with the two little girls, revolves symmetrically around the older drummer; and the left-hand group is disposed according to the system of "two plus three." Furthermore, some of the gestures are part of the balance of the composition. One example is the raised arms of the men that spread to the same extent as the skirts of their kilts.

In this ancient, well-assimilated wisdom there is, however, a new spirit — the urgent desire to render the momentary gesture. To this end the profile lines are broken, cadences crumble and there is some obvious slovenliness — in the central group of men, not all the arms are represented. But these are positive elements in this new mode of expression, in which any stylistic device has been employed to seize the immediate and the transitory by artists sated with the eternal perfection of the past.

SATIRICAL SCENE. *Dynasty XIX.*

In drawing, improvisation became part of the pictorial vocabulary of artists in the Ramessid age, as if they had discovered the pleasures of ordinary speech over the language of song and recitation. The artists' most direct expressions are seen in the notable series of virtuoso sketches that were

Satirical Scene
Dynasty XIX.
Colored drawing on papyrus; height 4″.

made on white limestone chips and terra-cotta sherds. In these, the artist's work is less an evocative rite and more an expression of state of mind and fantasy.

The same approach accounts for some extensive compositions on papyrus that are alien to the official repertory. They include erotic or topsy-turvy scenes, as when animals are shown in the guise of human beings. In this scene, we have a world in which the mice are the masters and the cats the servants. Perhaps there is a connection with contemporary animal fables. In this bizarre invention, the ordinary world is turned upside down.

FAIENCE BOWL. *Dynasty XIX.*

Egyptian faience — which is most often blue in color — consists of a friable, sandy paste of fireproof material held by a vitrified coating of siliceous varnish. Faience bowls have lively decorations, usually showing aquatic motifs. Not all the decorative elements are Egyptian, but the symmetry is more rigid than is normal. Themes from foreign handicrafts, imported into Egypt in the course of international trade, often appear in this industrial art. The two palmettos in this example belong to a motif imported from Syria.

Faience Bowl
Dynasty XIX; thirteenth century B.C.
Blue ceramic; diameter 7″.

141

FUNERARY PAPYRUS OF TA-DI-MUT, SINGER OF AMON. *Dynasty XXI.*

From the New Kingdom on, it was the custom to place in Egyptian tombs a collection of magic and religious formulas written on papyrus. In earlier times the pharaohs had these inscribed on the walls of the mortuary chamber. Later they were commonly inscribed on the coffin itself. These texts were intended to secure the protection of a certain number of divinities in the next world and to deflect the dangers that might be encountered there. They were also meant to allow the deceased to rise out of the tomb as he wished and in the form he preferred. Some of these papyruses from

Funerary Papyrus of Ta-di-Mut, Singer of Amon
Detail.
Dynasty XXI; tenth century B.C.
Colored drawing on papyrus; height 9".
From Thebes.

On pages 144–145: another detail from the papyrus.

the Eighteenth Dynasty have polychrome illustrations accompanying the text. This one is from the Twenty-first Dynasty tomb of Ta-di-Mut, singer of Amon, who was associated with the temple world of Thebes. There are scenes of the Elysian Fields — where it is a pleasure to work because of the wonderful harvests to be gathered, and where there is fresh water to drink. Geb, the god of the earth, in the form of a crocodile, looks on peacefully. The refinement of the composition, drawing, and color show what the tradition of official art was still capable of producing. Little has been touched by the revolutionary changes, but the position of the woman drinking, and even more the rendering of her disheveled hair, reveal the effects of the new inspiration.

GOLD PITCHER. *Dynasty XIX.*

This highly unusual piece was found by chance at Zagazig in 1907, during work on the railroad line. Found with it were numerous other gold and silver objects, ingots and scraps of precious metals, and a bracelet bearing the name of a granddaughter of Ramesses II. The random nature of the collection suggests that the objects may have been gathered for use or re-use in a goldsmith's shop. Since the find was made illegally, and the goods recovered only later, there is no precise dating for the excavation. The level at which the objects were found, however, is some sixty-five feet below the Roman strata.

The handle in the form of a goat on this pitcher is a familiar conception, as it was the practice to decorate metal vases with animal figures. It has been suggested that this type of object, and this pitcher in particular, had an Asian origin. The figure on the belly of the vase, who is in the act of worshiping Astarte or another Asian divinity, supports this view. But a long inscription in hieroglyphics, and the form of the vase — which was well-known in Egypt, except for the detail of the goat — cast doubt on any foreign origin. Furthermore, the owner, who is named in the inscription and described as "the king's envoy in all countries," may have been a connecting link between Syrian motifs and Egyptian craftsmanship. This precious vessel testifies to the wealth of cultural experience in Ramessid times.

Gold Pitcher
Dynasty XIX.
Gold and silver; height 7″, maximum diameter 7″.
From Tell Basta (Zagazig). (53262)

THE LATE AGE

Mentemhet the Governor
Ethiopian period; Dynasty XXV,
seventh century B.C.
Gray granite; height 4′ 5″.
From Thebes. (42236)

MENTEMHET THE GOVENOR. *Dynasty XXV.*

The Ramessid age saw the complete assimilation to traditional forms of the Amarna taste for the transitory. This experience was passed on to succeeding ages which reduced it to a languid hedonistic interest in elegant line. This had been exorcized by Tell el Amarna, but reappeared by devious routes in the works of art of the "Libyan" dynasty. This refinement of Egyptian culture elicited the political and cultural reaction of the sovereigns from Nubia who came to occupy Egypt. Among the barbarian populations of Nubia a mythologically pure sense of Egyptian tradition had been preserved, even though it had taken on much of African culture.

The last representative of these "Ethiopian" lords in Egypt was Mentemhet, governor of Thebes. He built a mortuary temple in his name and a significant number of monuments in other temples. His mortuary temple is one of the most interesting examples of archaeological art in Egypt. The various chambers are decorated in different styles, each representing a specific taste in representation. Similarly in the statues and other monuments of the governor, each in turn reflects a classical period in Egyptian art. This standing statue is a portrait of the governor. He is shown full-figure; the statue is heavily and classically composed.

BUST OF MENTEMHET THE GOVERNOR. *Dynasty XXV.*

Among the nostalgic throwbacks to the past in the Ethiopian period, the most vital pieces utilize Memphite and Middle Kingdom artistic themes,

Bust of Mentemhet the Governor
Ethopian period; Dynasty XXV.
Black granite; height 20″.
From the temple of Mut at Karnak.
(647)

whose immediate feeling for the compact and heavy mass coincided with the dominant taste of the Ethiopian period. In this portrait bust of Mentemhet, there is no pretence of achieving elegance. The return to a classical type as well as the deliberate roughness of expression are evidence of a new view in art. From this attitude, Saite Neoclassicism would later develop.

PORTRAIT OF IRIGADIGANEN. *Dynasty XXV.*

Another Ethiopian official is portrayed in this outstanding statue. The costume, more like a woman's than a man's, is perhaps an ethnic style of dress. Much more unusual is the hopeless, sagging obesity. Not since the colossi of Ikhnaton had there been such an emphasis on an unattractive body. The result is very different from what was sought in the earlier works. Here the obesity makes a coherent mass, similar to the broad hips, the heavy breasts and the elaborate round wigs of the feminine portraits of the time. This is the most realistic torso in Egyptian culture; the head is no less individual. A programmatic opposition to Egyptian elegance has been expressed here by an alert and venturesome sculptor, who is perhaps related to those artists around Mentemhet who knew how to tailor their expression to an antiquarian inspiration.

THE GOD OSIRIS. *Dynasty XXX.*

The statue is one of a group of monuments found at Sakkara in the tomb of Psammetichus, an official at the court of a king of the last native dynasty before the arrival of Alexander the Great. The god Osiris is shown wrapped in his shroud, from which his hands emerge. He is holding the insignia, and on his head he wears a complicated crown, called an *atef*. The principal merit of the statue lies in its finished workmanship. It represents a stand taken against the facile "improvisation" that was popular in Egyptian art from the Ramessid to the Bubastis period.

PSAMMETICHUS PROTECTED
BY THE COW HATHOR. *Dynasty XXX.* *p. 152*

Like the preceding work, this figure is from the tomb of Psammetichus at Sakkara. The finished workmanship, the sureness of the cutting, and the precision of the composition are notable. A comparison with *Amenophis II With The Cow of the Goddess Hathor,* which was probably the inspiration for this work, is legitimate and instructive. One grasps the cooling of the

form under the polished and confident surfaces, and the growing distance from the taste for reality as part of the inspiration. The imagination of the sculptor is evident in the chain around the animal's neck, a finished work that sets off the broad areas of the back and the belly. The validity of the artist's choice of inspiration led him to compete with the solid structural merits of the older models.

Psammetichus Protected by the Cow Hathor
Saite period; Dynasty XXX.
Green schist; length 3' 5".
From Sakkara. (784)

THE GRECO-ROMAN AGE

PORTRAIT OF A QUEEN. *Second Century B.C.*

The conquest of Egypt by Alexander the Great and the establishment of a center of Greek civilization at Alexandria, brought the country into close contact with Hellenistic culture. Prior contacts between the two cultures had been superficial and external; each civilization had continued to develop in its own traditions.

Aside from some eccentric fusions in the field of art, Greco-Egyptian culture found its expression in the social and religious spheres. The Ptolemies supported a considerable Egyptianizing activity in the arts, with the aim of creating an Egyptian base for their power. This allowed the old traditions to continue to develop, and thus one may speak of a Ptolemaic period in Egyptian art.

This statue of a queen is a good example of the artistic tendencies of the time. The aura of Saite art is still strong, as the perfection of the impersonal face shows. It is constructed according to the familiar scheme that consisted of eyebrows arched above the nose, horizontally placed eyes, compressed lips with two deep dimples at the corners, a round chin, and a full throat. The care in the execution of the details of the ears and the curly locks is also Saite in origin. Significantly, however, the work was modeled more on Ramessid than on more ancient Egyptian sculpture, and its parallels with *Funeral Procession* (page 138) are obvious. This turning away from the Memphite world is even more evident in the manner of treating the masses: the breasts are heavy and separated by deep shadow, while the hips and belly are rounded. The bent arm stresses the simplicity of the composition, and the branch held in the hand (a Ramessid iconographical detail) is a further element in the breaking up of light and shade. It was by resuscitating the vitality of the Egyptian "baroque" from Saite Neoclassicism that Hellenistic taste affected Egyptian tradition.

Portrait of a Queen
Ptolemaic period; second century B.C.
Painted limestone; height 28".
Provenance unknown. (678)

155

PORTRAIT OF PETOSIRIS. *Second Century B.C.*

The cultural cross-fertilization of Egypt and Greece led to works like this one from the Roman period. In typically Egyptian fashion a new problem has been interpreted in terms of traditions that continued to be respected. There is a desperate desire to save the vital sense of mass and structure — the one constant in a long history of resolving problems in representation.

Portrait of Petosiris
Egyptian-Roman period; second century B.C.
Black schist; height 33″.
From Memphis. (696)

Right: detail.

HEAD OF SERAPIS.

Along with the "Ptolemaic" solutions in Egyptian art in the Greek period, there were many works that were Hellenistic in inspiration. Hellenism centered on Alexandria, whose stylistic identity was marked by a taste for surface gradations that create a sensitive play of light. Alexandria saw the creation of a divinity imported into Egypt by Ptolemy II, with the assistance of an Egyptian priest and one of the Eumolpidae — Serapis, the Greek version of a form of Osiri-Hapi, who had the role of dynastic divinity of the Ptolemies as Lords of Egypt. The iconographic type was influenced by Phidias' Zeus, and included such details as the *modius,* a circlet in the form of a corn measure, which has disappeared from this example. It is obvious that even though it was created in Egypt, this statue is not part of Egyptian art. Indeed it shows how the artistic currents that coexisted in Egypt followed their own historic course.

Head of Serapis
Detail.
Hellenistic period.
Unpolished white marble; height 3′ 11″.
From Beni Masar. (46343)

Sacred Bull
Roman period; second century B.C.
Bronze; height 5″. (29357)

SACRED BULL. *Second Century B.C.*
The solar disk between the horns shows that this statue represents one of the sacred bulls of Egypt. The ancient animal cults did not become an important part of Egyptian life until later times, when they attracted the attention of foreign visitors and, in particular, aroused the indignation of the Romans. Nevertheless, this bronze figurine from the Roman period is not Egyptian in type. It is merely an adaptation to an exotic world (the solar disk) of one of the little animal figures that were a common product of contemporary industrial art.

HEAD OF AN EMPEROR. *Circa A.D. 300.*

The confident stylization of the features, the solid construction, the aggressive look, and the wrinkles characterize this anonymous masterpiece from the period immediately before Constantine. If there is any Egyptian element in the portrait, it is only the Oriental strain common to all late classical art. After this time, "Egyptian" art gave way to more ecumenical modes of expression. And with the establishment of Coptic art, Egypt gained a variation of the Byzantine mode of seeing and interpreting.

Head of an Emperor
Roman period; circa A.D. 300.
Red porphyry; height 23″.
From Benha. (962)

HISTORY OF THE MUSEUM
AND ITS BUILDING

The romantic circumstances behind the foundation of the Egyptian Museum in Cairo form a chapter in art history that reads like a thriller. The reconstruction of ancient Egyptian civilization, which was the work of European scholars, took place during a colonial period. Egypt at the time was socially depressed, and only much later would obtain national independence and a greater awareness of its own archaeological past.

The creation of the major museums of Europe and America was in response to a growing interest in the visual arts and to the general cultural heritage typical of Western civilization in the nineteenth century. But the foundation of a museum of Egyptian antiquities in Cairo was literally sabotaged for more than half a century by private interests with a stake in maintaining their monopoly of the highly lucrative trade in archaeological objects, and by the indifference of the government to the history of ancient Egypt and the protection of its treasures. A Museum was finally established thanks to the exceptional tenacity of a famous French archaeologist, Auguste Mariette, who dedicated his life to the realization of this project. His success came too late, however, to save an incalculable amount of material which had already gone to European collections.

The fate of the Museum, and to a certain extent of Egyptology itself, was from the beginning tied to French political hegemony in Egypt during the last century. One of the more interesting parts of the "Empire Style," the Egyptian mode became popular after Napoleon's famous campaign in 1798–99. Before then, European knowledge of Egyptian art was limited to the objects and figurines that were displayed as exotic pieces in curio cabinets and collections. Following Napoleon's expedition, collectors all over the world began to compete to buy such pieces, and even large monumental works. Consequently, in the first thirty years of the nineteenth century there was a continuous outflow of antiquities, much of which went to form the bases of the great Egyptian collections in the major European museums. This dispersion was aided by the foreign ambassadors in Cairo and was tolerated by the Pashas, who considered the antiquities their private property which could be dispensed in the form of personal gifts to influential foreigners.

The only serious objection to these depredations came from the eminent French scholar Champollion, who petitioned Mohammad Ali in 1830 to create a local conservation and preservation station for antiquities. This request was ignored until a banal diplomatic incident induced the Pasha to take measures against the exportation of objects by establishing a government service and a museum, which were housed in a school building by the Ezbekiah Pool. In 1835, the director, Youssef Zia Effendi, started an inspection campaign in Middle Egypt, while Linant Bey was assigned the task of drawing up an inventory of the ancient sites and moving the most precious objects to the museum. The results were not impressive, and the collection amassed was small. In the mid-nineteenth century some pieces from the excavations of Serapeum were added to the exhibits, but in 1855 the Pasha made a present of the entire collection to the Archduke Maximilian of Austria, who happened to be visiting Cairo, and so the first Museum in Cairo ended up in Vienna.

It was at this low point that Auguste Mariette exerted his influence. Formerly an assistant in the Department of Egyptian Art at the Louvre, he went to Egypt in 1850 to acquire Coptic manuscripts and remained there to do his own excavations and at first took part himself in the trade in ancient objects. During that first stay, however, he became convinced of the need for a proper local museum. Mariette returned to Egypt in 1857, and with the support of the French government as well as de Lesseps' influence with the Pasha, he was appointed Director of Antiquities in 1858. This assignment did not call for the foundation of a Museum, nor for a regular salary, but it gave a man as ambitious as Mariette the chance to use his wits. He set to work at once on the urgent job of documenting the ruins, and obtained quarters for storing the objects from the first excavations. The old offices of a river-transport company on the Nile at Boulak were the first home of the future Cairo Museum. Mariette moved in with his family and arranged four exhibition rooms, which he decorated with his own wall paintings.

The popularity of this little collection convinced the Pasha of the importance of his treasures. The selection of a site and the allocation of funds for a proper museum were being debated when Said Pasha died in 1863. His successor, Ismail, had a more ambitious plan for a much larger institution that would house not only the greatly enlarged collection of the little museum at Boulak but also Greek antiquities and Arab art. A new building in the neo-Egyptian style, with a garden for displaying sculpture, was inaugurated in 1863. When Mariette died in 1881, his dream had been largely realized. The results of the excavations had aroused the enthusiasm of Europe when they were shown at the international exhibitions in London in 1862 and in Paris in 1867. A flood had badly damaged the Boulak Museum in 1878, but five years earlier the project of building a grandiose museum in Cairo had been undertaken, and the Antiquities Service had become a regular part of the government administration.

THE BUILDING

After being moved to the Giza Palace in 1891, the collections were definitively installed in the present building at Midan El-Tahreer in 1902. Marcel Dourgnon, a French architect who won the international competition for the new Museum, designed the structure but died before his plans were carried out.

During the last fifty years, the original collection has been increased by impressive discoveries, such as the tomb of Tutankhamon in 1922, whose contents comprise one of its most magnificent sections. The

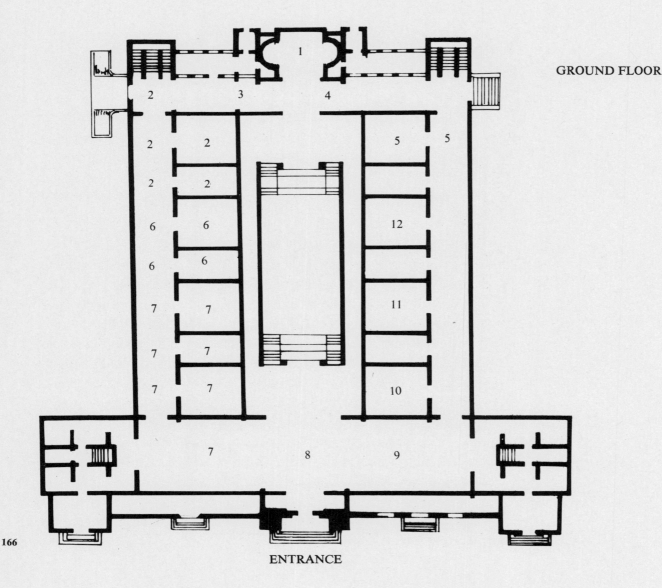

GROUND FLOOR

ENTRANCE

building has been progressively altered and enlarged to house its vast possessions, which range from prehistory to Egyptian art under the Roman occupation.

As described in the Introduction, the works are displayed in chronological order. Today the Museum, which has been strongly supported by the present government, is under the Ministry of Culture, which directs the Antiquities Service, maintains the Museum, publishes its catalogues, and sponsors traveling exhibitions of its treasures.

FIRST FLOOR

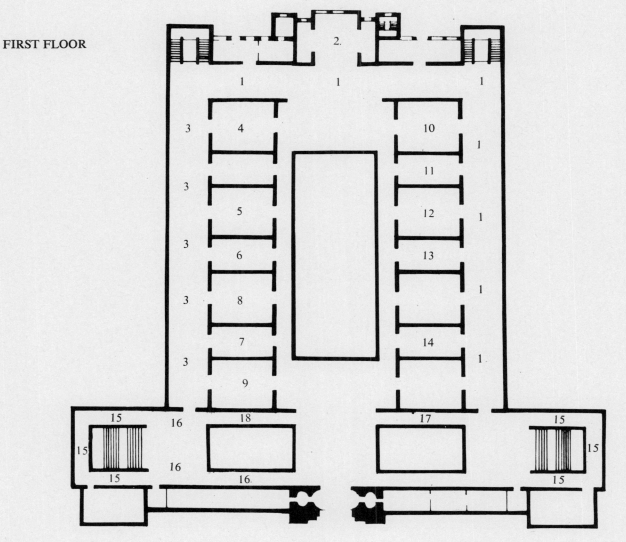

SELECTED BIBLIOGRAPHY

ALDRED, CYRIL. *Development of Ancient Egyptian Art, 3200–1315 B.C.* (Tiranti, London, 1952).

BOULANGER, ROBERT. *Egyptian Painting and the Ancient East.* (Funk and Wagnalls, New York, 1965).

COTTRELL, LEONARD. *The Horizon Book of Lost Worlds.* (American Heritage, New York, 1962).

DAVIES, NINA. *Egyptian Tomb Painting.* (London, 1953).

DRIOLON, ETIENNE. *Egyptian Art.* (Golden Griffin Books, New York, 1950).

FAIRSERVIS, JR., WALTER A. *The Ancient Kingdoms of the Nile.* (Thomas Y. Crowell Co., New York, 1962).

FAKHRY, AHMED. *The Pyramids.* (University of Chicago Press, Chicago, 1961).

LANGE, KURT and MAX HIRMER. *Egypt: Architecture, Sculpture, Painting in Three Thousand Years.* (Phaidon, New York, 1968).

MACQUITTY, WILLIAM. *Abu Simbel.* (G. P. Putnam's Sons, New York, 1965).

MEKHITARIAN, ARPAG. *Egyptian Painting.* (Skira, Geneva, 1954).

PRITCHARD, JAMES. *The Ancient Near East in Pictures.* (Princeton University Press, Princeton, 1954).

SMITH, WILLIAM S. *The Art and Architecture of Ancient Egypt.* (London, 1966).

WOLDERING, IRMGARD. *The Art of Egypt: The Time of the Pharaohs.* (Crown Publishers, New York, 1965).

INDEX OF ILLUSTRATIONS

INDEX OF NAMES

GENERAL INDEX